EDITOR MISSING

EDITOR MISSING

THE MEDIA IN TODAY'S INDIA

RUBEN BANERJEE

HarperCollins *Publishers* India

First published in India by HarperCollins Publishers 2022
4th Floor, Tower A, Building No. 10, Phase II, DLF Cyber City,
Gurugram, Haryana –122002
www.harpercollins.co.in

2 4 6 8 10 9 7 5 3 1

Copyright © Ruben Banerjee 2022

P-ISBN: 978-93-9440-746-6
E-ISBN: 978-93-9440-747-3

The views and opinions expressed in this book are the author's own.
The facts are as reported by him and the publishers
are not in any way liable for the same.

Ruben Banerjee asserts the moral right
to be identified as the author of this work.

All rights reserved. No part of this publication may be reproduced, stored in a retrieval system, or transmitted, in any form or by any means, electronic, mechanical, photocopying, recording or otherwise, without the prior permission of the publishers.

Typeset in 11.5/16 Bembo Std at
Manipal Technologies Limited, Manipal

Printed and bound at
Thomson Press (India) Ltd

This book is produced from independently certified FSC® paper
to ensure responsible forest management.

To

Deepali Banerjee
My Ma – who too left us like Baba

CONTENTS

PREFACE

I WISH I DIDN'T HAVE TO WRITE THIS BOOK. AT LEAST NOT SO SOON. You tend to reminisce about your past only when the present has seemingly overtaken you and the future doesn't seem to hold much hope. I consider this book – part memoir – a bit premature. However, a sudden disruption that threatened to derail my career occurred, which was least expected. I didn't bargain for it either. But far from doom and gloom, the changed circumstances presented a rare opportunity. I suddenly had the privilege of having a lot of spare time for undisturbed contemplation. The result is this book, something that I certainly had not planned for at this point.

But before putting pen to paper, there was a lot to ponder over. For one, I am not half as well-known as many of my fellow journalists and I certainly do not fit into the category of celebrity editors who crowd our consciousness. On the contrary, my career – though long – has been considerably less remarkable than that of many of my contemporaries who are high-profile journalists. True,

I have worked diligently and honestly, and have also often found myself in the middle of conflicts and calamities. But I haven't covered any wars and have never carried out any stings. I have not done TV journalism and my face is in no way famous.

Yet, not everything about me was ordinary. Call it destiny or a stroke of luck; I did get to occupy a chair once occupied by no less than the legendary editor Vinod Mehta. As his latter-day successor at one of India's best-known news magazines, I got a ringside view of the tumult that constantly defines a vast country as ours. From my perch as the editor of *Outlook*, I gained a wholly different perspective. Good or bad, the constant churnings shaped our collective fortune and possibly left us more divided.

While not necessarily in the thick of things, I watched them closely. They gave me deep insights and helped me better understand issues – from politics to the market and ideological forces at play that adversely impact the media. They impacted the calls that I took as an editor, and finally influenced the direction that my career took. The experiences I had were certainly enriching. But just when I thought that they had made me wiser, I found myself poorer without a regular job. The following pages are an account of the kaleidoscope of the terrific highs and terrifying lows that marked my life. Each one of them, I believe, have important takeaways for those trying to make better sense of present-day India. If not anything else, they can serve as cautionary tales for journalists who would be required to negotiate plenty of professional and political pitfalls.

In more ways than one, this book – rich in anecdotes and real-life instances – should prove to be useful. Particularly since it comes at a time when almost everything in this country is fiercely contested, and we are grappling to come to terms with deep divisions that run through us. At no point in the past have we perhaps lived in such trying times, despite our tryst with the Emergency in the mid-1970s. Among the very many things that we find upsetting, what roils a sizeable section of us the most these days, is perhaps the perceived shrinking space for free speech. We are less tolerant of contrarian views. The right to dissent that should be the bedrock of any decent democracy is believed to be seriously endangered in India. There are many who, consequently, feel we are in the midst of an undeclared and worst form of Emergency.

But unanimity is sorely missing from our lexicon; not everyone agrees with the dark parallels currently drawn with our past. The jury is consequently out on the current state of health of the world's largest democracy. In fact, when Prime Minister Narendra Modi described it as the 'mother of all democracies' during his September 2021 visit to the US, it only triggered another raucous round of disagreements. Those in his favour hailed the statement while those against dismissed it as hollow rhetoric. As charges and counter-charges fly on almost anything and everything that dominates public discourse, with no consensus anywhere in sight, we are undeniably becoming more divided and polarized.

This tell-all book relying on reflections of my eventful editorship at *Outlook* as well as my earlier stints as a fledgling reporter struggling to make his mark seeks to tell the intriguing story of contemporary India in an honest manner. The media, they say, mirrors society – warts and all. In India, however, it has been in the news mostly for all the wrong reasons. Journalists are supposed to be objective, tasked with telling every side of a story. They are also meant to be free, fearless and not favouring anyone. But the reality is a far cry from what journalists – the pillars of the fourth estate – originally stood for. A divided polity has meant an equally divided media. One section never tires of unabashedly batting for those in power while the other spares no effort in criticizing the establishment. With battle lines so clearly drawn, there is growing concern that truth could be, and often is, the casualty.

Though not exactly a paragon of virtue with several inherent flaws pockmarking my own persona, I, as a journalist, haven't ever swung to extreme positions. Call me old school or old-fashioned; I have been a centrist all my life, preferring to call a spade a spade unencumbered by political likes or dislikes. My personal beliefs or choices haven't ever coloured my journalism. Further, my stint as an editor did give me the rare privilege of taking a closer look at what could be the best obtainable version of the truth. Every time something big happened, triggering more divisions and debates, I got to look at them as an impartial observer. I tried as much as humanly possible not to be partisan in my views and get to the bottom of issues. I dare not say what I concluded and what *Outlook* reported were the ultimate truth. But our reportage was indeed unburnished and unbiased, even if not universally liked.

We held on to our ground and scruples as much as we could. That was also the case when *Outlook* did its much talked about 'Missing' cover in May 2021. It was the time when the country was being singed by a debilitating second surge of Covid, resulting in deaths and desolation on an unparalleled scale. We calculated the potential costs of putting out such a cover that had every chance of becoming controversial. It did, but never did we flinch as journalists in pursuing what was only the right course. We never wished to be complicit in the large-scale deaths and instead chose to call out what we considered a near abdication of its responsibilities by the government of the day. In an interview with CNN in the wake of the cover, I preferred to call it an act of obligation and not bravery. This book details the consequences of what I believe will be judged by history as a fine example of our undying faith in living up to one's call of duty.

Defending truth can exact unintended costs, and the behind-the-scene story of our 'Missing' cover serves as an eloquent testimony of it. It was the perfect culmination of collective teamwork – I thought about the idea, several of my colleagues commissioned the articles, and someone else came up with the actual 'Missing' title, which for all purposes set the cat among the pigeons. But it has come to define my editorship, and some have gone a step ahead to declare it as a shot at writing my own legacy. But legacy or not, I am reeling from the shockwaves it undeniably set off, and I can safely say it has not been comforting.

While I could just have been collateral damage, *Outlook*'s 'Missing' cover exemplified the challenges that confront the media in India today. Brickbats and bouquets followed in equal measure, underscoring the pain points of pursuing balanced and objective journalism in a fractious polity. There was even a plot to portray us as foot soldiers of a particular political party. Friends turned foes while those who never considered us on their side suddenly became the loudest votaries of what we said on our cover. Everyone did what suited them the best, and the country's fault lines were further exposed. It also set off a chain of events, which served as a rude awakening to the challenges posed by the current circumstances. And the cost of speaking out turned out to be pretty high.

This book is not a cradle-to-graveyard story of a journalist who could be in the twilight of his career. Rather, it seeks to understand how deep the rot is in journalism in India and whether the profession is redeemable. Is there any possibility of the profession rediscovering its principles? More importantly, what are the underlying reasons for the media to have become so divided and often so unscrupulous?

The following pages are replete with the depiction of the harsh realities that await us at every turn of life. From being dismissively asked to fetch tea by a prospective employer at the beginning of my career to being feted as an editor towards the end, I have had my share of ups and downs. The close shaves that I have had – from a bomb blast just metres away that claimed some two dozen lives in Guwahati to a near-disaster when an invective was mischievously printed in place of a prominent Union minister's identity – added drama and excitement. This is where the true significance of this book lies. The resultant lessons from them would expectedly be relevant as well. I hope they resonate with starry-eyed young journalists, who have set their sights on a life-long journey into the world of fair, objective and impartial journalism. If any lessons are learnt from my experience, this book's purpose would have been served. And I will consider myself a proud claimant of some worthy credit.

1

UNCOVERING THE COVER

ALL HELL BROKE LOOSE SUDDENLY THAT THURSDAY. WITHIN HALF-an-hour after I had tweeted[1] the cover of the 24 May 2021 issue of *Outlook*, it appeared that my short and succinct social media post had touched a raw nerve. Though not exactly a Twitter star, I had a fair idea of how Twitter worked – having had the occasional taste of my posts going viral or being savagely trolled in the past. Praise and criticism being the norm in the social media space, nothing usually surprised me. But this Thursday was different. The response to my tweet was fast and furious. In some ways, it was fierce, too, as some of the feedback turned angry and abusive.

I was shaken despite being supremely confident that we had put to bed the previous night an exceptionally good issue of the news magazine. Shepherded in earlier times by the irreverent and fearless Vinod Mehta, the weekly had the reputation of being bold and brave. Standing up to and taking on those in power without the fear of consequences had been a part of its DNA. For me, the latest issue of the magazine was not charting new territory, but only living up to its exalted pedigree – albeit under changed circumstances.

Yet, the manner in which a section of the Twitterati responded to my announcement of the issue found me unprepared. In the strictest sense, I was stunned and possibly speechless.

My phone began to buzz and did not stop ringing. Text messages crammed my inbox. Those reaching out were friends, friends' friends and even *Outlook* colleagues who worked in other departments and had nothing to do with the editorial choices we made. I suddenly found myself being hailed as a hero and feted for what they said was exemplary courage. But it wasn't I alone who fielded effusively complimentary calls and messages. My daughter began to receive calls as well from her college mates in Bengaluru. They had already changed their display images on Twitter and WhatsApp to the *Outlook* cover. Hundreds of unknown others reached out to me on Twitter to inform me that they were doing the same. Suddenly, the exceptionally minimalistic *Outlook* cover that was uncharacteristically sparse both in the use of letters and imagery was the talk of the town. It made the loudest statement.

In between the barrage of congratulatory calls, there were calls of concern too. Will I be okay? Have I contemplated the 'consequences'? Those who knew me intimately and genuinely cared for my well-being called intermittently. All this while my original Twitter post gathered further steam. More and more people retweeted it. Never to miss an opportunity, politicians who found my tweet convenient joined in. They amplified it further, adding their own remarks. To say my tweet had gone viral was an understatement. It was nothing short of an avalanche.

I should have been on cloud nine, soaking in my sudden tryst with fame, however transient. But amidst the volley of fulsome praise landed a WhatsApp message that carried a somewhat ominous ring. 'Dada, are you really printing this cover?' – messaged my old friend and influential Union minister, Dharmendra Pradhan. I have known Dharmendra since I was a cub reporter and he was a student dabbling in student politics. We went back a long way – decades – since my time, first as an *Indian Express* reporter and then as an *India Today* correspondent, in Orissa (now spelt Odisha). We were genuinely proud of each other. Our admiration was mutual – that he had grown to become a Union minister was a matter of pride for me. Though the two of us made for a silent mutual admiration club, we kept our distance. We occasionally spoke to each other – perhaps once every three or four months – but rarely met.

But we were accessible to each other, and Dharmendra that Thursday morning was reaching out to check the veracity of what he had been asked to find out by his party. I guessed what he was trying to get at. There have been too many occasions in the recent past when covers of prominent magazines, including foreign ones such as *Time*, had been forged and circulated. Some of them caricatured Prime Minister Narendra Modi or viciously censured him. That being the case, it was natural for Dharmendra – Muku to me by his nickname – to figure out if the latest *Outlook* cover, widely in circulation on social media, was genuine. By the time his message landed, I was a bit overwhelmed. As against the normal practice, I took my time to respond. In a way, I was also buying time. Having sent the magazine to the printing press well past midnight, I calculated that by now copies of the magazine were being possibly sent to our chain of distributors and agents for their onward journey to retailers, vendors and stands. I had no intention of disrupting the supply chain.

I sat on a reply deliberately for a couple of hours. And when I was reasonably certain that the copies had been distributed, I replied. 'Yes, this is the cover of the next issue.' Prompt came the response. 'Unfortunate'. It was abundantly clear that the latest cover with the word 'MISSING' written in bold across it had greatly riled him. That the leaders of the political party that he belonged to would be unhappy as well wasn't difficult to guess.

Facing a backlash has always been part of my journalistic existence and that our latest cover wouldn't make everyone happy wasn't unexpected. Yet, I was somewhat stumped by the scale and intensity of the feedback that a mere announcement had received. Given our news cycle, Thursdays were meant to be a kind of a relaxed day with the magazine having gone to press the previous night, or as it often happened, in the wee hours of the morning. Everyone in the edit team took it easy after days of intense work. I, too, normally looked forward to slumping myself on my favourite sofa and stretching my legs. It was the best day of the week for a family outing or a leisurely lunch with friends. With the next issue at least seven days away, Thursdays were meant to be stress-free.

This Thursday, however, rapidly turned tense, though I was sanguine about the fact that we had a great issue. It had an unusually strong editorial. But more importantly, it featured exclusive columns by some of the biggest names in the country, such as Pratap Bhanu Mehta, Shashi Tharoor and Manoj Kumar Jha. We also had our team of brilliant reporters dissecting the performance of the government during its seven-year tenure. Overall, it was power-packed with all that one needed: incisive analysis, commentary and strong ground reporting that provided a no-nonsense perspective.

Ironically, my doubts about the response the issue would evoke stemmed from the certainty that it was a killer issue. For one, I wasn't sure how the promoters of *Outlook* would take it. Some three years ago, when they had decided to hire me as editor, and for which I remain eternally grateful, they had given an inkling of what they had in mind. After several rounds of conversations spread over at least four months, I finally got to meet the family patriarch – Rajan Raheja – at their penthouse on the top floor of the glass-fronted Raheja Towers in Mumbai's upscale Santa Cruz.

Once considered among the fifty richest men in the country – going by a *Forbes* magazine report – he ran a business empire that straddled several sectors, from real estate to hotels and a chain of stores. Exide, the automobile battery that powers most vehicles on Indian roads, is also owned by the branch of the Raheja clan headed by Rajan. But in my meeting with him in April 2018, with his two sons – Akshay and Viren – in attendance, he betrayed no sense of the influence and wealth that he commanded. As polite as one could be, he prodded me about my political beliefs and how I would, if chosen, navigate a magazine during increasingly polarized times.

Out to impress him, I said what I thought would be seen as correct. But then I wasn't trying to pull a fast one. I stayed truthful all the while, prompted by my own convictions. Neither a supporter of the Bharatiya Janata Party (BJP) nor of the Congress, I held forth on what I believed would be the right course for any publication: being a centrist with fairness, balance and objectivity as the guiding principles. Never under the illusion of being a paragon of virtue – ask my wife and daughter, and they would tell you what my flaws are – I said what I truly believed in.

I buttressed what I said with arguments that I thought made sense. To me, taking political sides would be committing suicide. Credibility would be the first casualty, and I saw no reason why a magazine should take one side over the other. To me, what made more compelling sense was to be on the side of truth, or what we believed was the best obtainable version of the truth. I also strongly made a case for 'all-sides journalism', that we shouldn't blank out one side and give a platform to the others or vice-versa. On the contrary, I argued that we should give space to everyone on the spectrum of views, so long as they didn't incite violence or were blatantly abusive. But I did say that while ensuring balanced coverage, we should be entitled and free to take our own editorial stand.

Rajan Raheja, it seemed, liked what I said. He agreed with me, realizing that I was neither an activist nor an adventurist who would risk the magazine's existence to push my own beliefs or agenda. For that matter, I told him that these were trying times and we should be extra cautious in what we do. He nodded enthusiastically when I said that one could do journalism only if one's publication existed. If there is no magazine, there is no journalism for *Outlook* journalists, I said, emphasizing on the need to be clever in how we pursued our craft without compromising our principles.

Given his rapt attention, I knew the job was mine. And then he broke into what I presumed was Sindhi – his mother tongue – to talk briefly to his two sons. I sat there quietly, waiting for the verdict. But I knew it would be in my favour. After some time, Raheja finally turned to me, smiled, and said I was being hired as the editor of *Outlook*. He asked me to sit down with his sons to finalize the terms. As we stood up to go to an adjoining room, he said something that seemed to be the red line that he was drawing for me. 'Magazine *aap ka*, so take care of it. But yes! Be careful about the two. We shouldn't get into trouble.' His voice trailed off as we trooped out.

Raheja didn't spell out who the 'two' were. Neither did I ask. But it seemed we all knew to whom he was referring. I just nodded. As long as I could be truthful and not compromise on reporting the truth, it was fine. I could live with being extra cautious, a little more circumspect. The red line laid out before me did not alarm me.

As a matter of fact, the mantra of being over-cautious was of great help. For most of the little over three years I helmed *Outlook*, we did whatever we had to do and hit the right buttons. The BJP and the Congress played politics with the religious faith and tradition tied to the Sabarimala pilgrimage, and we called their bluff in a December 2018 issue of *Outlook*. We put the story on the cover. When Kashmir happened – no less than a surgical strike that saw the region stripped of its special status and downgraded into two union territories in August 2019 – we reported without fear or favour. For that matter, we followed up on the first anniversary of the repeal of Article 370 and did another cover, dissecting what India had gained or lost. Our covers – week after week – were loud statements. We reported the way we were expected to.

That I was in neither the BJP nor the Congress camp helped. We approached stories purely on merit and dealt with them accordingly.

My mantra as editor was to report to the best of our ability, but at the same time I didn't wish to draw unwelcome attention. When we did, they were backed by compelling reasons. For example, the 2019 general elections that Prime Minister Modi spectacularly won, silencing critics and disappointing all those who expected a different result. It was a particularly abrasive election marked by increased polarization. Barely weeks before the polls, *Time* magazine[2] famously put Modi on its cover and did a story that was widely talked about. Modi was controversially described as the 'Divider-in-Chief', and the accompanying story was unusually harsh. The *Time* issue divided the fractured nation further.

Once the results of the general elections were declared, it was clear that Modi was the tallest leader in Indian politics, whose popularity remained unmatched in the country. We respected the verdict and refused to let our personal biases get in the way. The issue of *Outlook* immediately after the results noted Modi's stupendous feat and had him on the cover. And in hailing him as the victor, we did not mince words. Our cover had a happy Modi with folded hands doing a grateful namaste. Underneath, we proclaimed him – in an interesting play of words prompted by the earlier *Time* cover –'Conqueror-in-Chief'.

Never to shy away from giving credit where it was due, the *Outlook* issue next week lingered on the BJP's spectacular electoral victory. This time, we had both Modi and home minister Amit Shah on the cover with the headline: 'JUGALBANDI'. In the articles that made up the cover package, we looked at how and why the BJP won and the roles the two leaders played in stitching together an electoral success. Always on the lookout for being different in our coverage, we had something extra. The main essay was written by a BJP insider: Dr Anirban Ganguly. As director of the Dr Syama Prasad Mookerjee Research Foundation – a BJP think tank – Ganguly evidently knew how the party had plotted and executed its poll strategy. In his piece,[3] Ganguly wrote what he wrote. While we agreed with some, we didn't agree with the rest. Yet, we provided him the platform since we felt the BJP's electoral showing had rightfully earned them a spot in the sun. They could say what they wished to without being censored. My basic journalistic principle of being fair and balanced had been burnished, I thought. I was wrong.

A month had not passed since the election results, when those who see nothing right with Modi and the BJP began to regain their voices that had been temporarily silenced by the poll reverses. One such person wrote an article on a media website, complaining that magazines in the country were being blatantly preferential in their treatment of Modi. He went on to cite examples: till the beginning of July that year, *India Today*, he claimed, had Modi on the cover – alone or with some other leaders – at least ten times. That made up 41.6 per cent of their twenty-four-odd covers for that year. The author cited the magazine *Open* as well, saying that they, in fact, had Modi alone on the cover an equal number of times during the period.

Since being under the radar was my motto, I was relieved that *Outlook* got off lightly, finding only a passing mention. *Outlook*, in comparison, had only two covers with Modi during this period, the author mentioned. I thought the numbers cited portrayed us and our journalism in a good light. But not exactly. Reshmi Dasgupta, journalist and wife of BJP Rajya Sabha member of parliament Swapan Dasgupta, chose to turn the numbers against us. In a tweet[4], she argued that there was nothing wrong in *India Today* and *Open* devoting so many covers to Modi. Instead, *Outlook* should be asked why it had done so few, she contended.

I ducked the query, reluctant to join issue and court an unnecessary controversy. Swapan had been my boss in my younger days, and I continue to hold him in respect for his immeasurable contributions in shaping my career. I also did not wish our journalism to come under partisan scrutiny. I was convinced we couldn't win such an argument.

In the run-up to the 'Missing' cover, I must confess, I had been worrying a bit. The first three years with *Outlook* had been a breeze. We did what we wanted to do, without being in the face or without calling anyone names. The magazine, going by feedback and what we genuinely felt, was again buzzing. It had turned unmistakably topical as we tackled what was relevant, controversial and even esoteric, with equal ease and minus any hindrance. Unlike the newsroom where I worked before *Outlook*, the Rahejas didn't interfere. I alone decided what the cover should be, and no one else called the shots, though my other editors were actively encouraged and empowered to challenge my choice. But once decided – the final call squarely rested with me – none stood in the way. The management implicitly trusted the decisions I took.

But did I violate their trust this time with the 'Missing' cover? The thought crossed my mind repeatedly even as I sought to convince myself that what we had done was the right thing to do. And why not?

However clichéd, journalists are known to be the fourth pillar of democracy – the watchdogs of society. It is for us to speak truth to power – in *Outlook*'s case, somewhat tactfully – and show the mirror to them too. The bottom line was that we had to speak up when the situation demanded it.

Ever since the deadly Covid-19 virus went on the rampage, our lives have been dramatically turned upside down. From March 2020, the pandemic had held us hostage, ebbing and flowing with time. Many among us paid with their lives, but life continued nevertheless, despite a hard lockdown that suddenly paused everything that we were accustomed to doing, causing great despair and distress. Then we got out of it, and the lockdown was gradually lifted and eased. Life showed signs of coming back on track and, tragically, we dropped our guard, comforted in no small measure by what our leaders chose to say and do in public.

Addressing a global meet in early 2021, Prime Minister Modi all but declared victory over the virus, claiming to the rest of the world that India was a shining example of Covid management. The world should look up to us to see how best to overcome the virus, Modi said in his trademark oratorial style.[5] Not to be outdone, the then Union health minister, Dr Harsh Vardhan, also chipped in with his share of wisdom.[6] 'The virus is in its end game here', he boasted a few weeks later, boosting our confidence further.

As the number of Covid patients in the country rapidly declined – and mortality figures stayed inexplicably low – our hopes soared. We went back to our unfettered lifestyle with gusto. Some went to the extent of describing it as 'revenge lifestyle'. Deprived of the freedoms that we were forced to give up because of the restrictions that the pandemic imposed, we revelled in rediscovering what we thought were our lost luxuries and privileges. Shops and markets reopened. Offices started functioning again and we got back to socializing and partying as if nothing was ever amiss. We had clearly not learnt any lessons.

All the while, the virus lurked dangerously close, without anyone noticing it. A few experts cautioned periodically about the dangers of being lax, but India moved into a triumphant mood, having mistaken the lull in the pandemic as permanent victory. Significantly, our politicians were among those who showed little concern. Assembly elections were underway in phases in several states, including in West Bengal, and they undertook crowded campaigns with seemingly no care in the world. At a time when social distancing ought to have been the norm, the Prime Minister, in fact, extolled the large turnout at one particular election rally in Bengal. Wah! What a crowd, he said to rapturous applause from a jostling audience, many of whom did not even wear the customary mask.[7]

Around the same time came the Kumbh Mela, and those in power and entrusted with our well-being chose to throw caution to the wind and allowed the congregation of tens of thousands of pilgrims. The virus was allowed a free run. In no time, it was at its rampaging peak and the nation's capital, Delhi, was firmly in its deadly grip. People started falling sick and there was a rush for hospital beds and ICUs. More and more people began suffering from acute symptoms. Their oxygen levels dropped – sometimes precariously – and they started suffocating. They needed oxygen support, but oxygen was in short supply. Many died excruciatingly painful and slow deaths. As both the numbers of patients and deaths rose, panic set in, and city after city, including Delhi, clamped lockdowns. Once again, we found ourselves homebound and helpless.

Cooped up in our homes, the *Outlook* editorial staff worked hard and tirelessly. We worked the phones and held virtual editorial conferences and decided to run a cover on the sickening situation. By then, the circumstances were dire and we ran a cover with the word 'Abandoned', summing up our helpless state. The 3 May 2021 issue documented the distress and despair that was dominating our lives. We all were seemingly adrift on a sea of helplessness, not certain when the virus would strike or what the future held. It was precisely then that the frightening reality that we were reporting hit home. First my wife, then my daughter and then I contracted Covid one after the other.

Grounded by the virus, we waited anxiously for a possible apocalypse. As fever came and went, we stayed riveted to the oximeters, continuously measuring our oxygen saturation levels. A thousand debilitating thoughts crossed our helpless minds during those long, dark nights as we stayed awake wondering whether our luck – and, more importantly, our oxygen levels – would hold. We knew if the oxygen saturation level in our blood dropped drastically, we possibly would not survive and would end up at a crematorium. People all around were dropping dead – at home, in parking lots of hospitals and in ambulances that ferried them in a frantic race to get timely hospital admission – and there seemed to be no hope. As we held our breaths, a friend we knew began showing acute Covid symptoms. He complained of breathlessness, and his oxygen level dropped alarmingly, well below eighty-five. His wife made frantic calls, as did I, to try and get some help. I called the staff of a Union minister to enquire if they could pull strings and help secure a bed in any hospital. The hassled staff promised to get back but never did. I tried my contacts in Lucknow, too, hoping they could possibly get a bed in the national capital region close to Delhi but under the administrative control of Uttar Pradesh. There, too, I found no luck.

Thankfully, my friend survived. First, he managed to get an oxygen cylinder on the black market at a steep premium. Then a rather enterprising contact got him a hospital bed, where he stayed for several weeks before fully recovering. We, too, turned out to be lucky. Covid spared us rather lightly. We all had our share of cough, cold, fever and body aches, but none in our family choked. We lived.

Our horrifying experience scarred us. Apart from being weak and exhausted, we were upset and angry. What made me angrier still was the manner in which those in power were seeking to deny the undeniable reality that had been forced upon us. The usually effusive Prime Minister was surprisingly quiet, while his cabinet colleagues continued to claim that nothing was wrong. Even as hospital after hospital reported[8] oxygen shortages that reportedly forced them to take patients off life support and let them die,[9] our government chose to be in denial. The government in Delhi, headed by Aam Aadmi Party's Arvind Kejriwal, claimed acute shortage in the supply of oxygen. Its claim, however, was contested by officials of the Central government with BJP at the helm. In court and outside, they engaged in fierce debate about how much oxygen Delhi actually needed. That people were dying for want of it never deterred them.[10]

Adequately angry, I perhaps needed a spark to light the fuse for discarding my customary caution. It came in the shape of the 17 May 2021 issue of the *India Today* magazine that I happened to see on a Friday. 'A Failed State' the magazine proclaimed provocatively on its cover that had the powerful image of a long queue of bodies in a crematorium. The issue had me worked up.

Outlook's rivalry with *India Today* had a long history, with the latter ruling the roost unchallenged till *Outlook* came on the scene in 1995. *Outlook*, then under its founding editor Vinod Mehta, started as a weekly, instantly putting the market leader and more established *India Today* under pressure. Fabled as an extremely agile editor with a pulse on what the readers wanted, Mehta had several aces up his sleeve and the inaugural issue of *Outlook* was a big hit. It did what was hitherto unthinkable, putting on its cover an opinion poll on what Kashmiris thought about their place in India. The findings of the poll were startling, and *Outlook* went to town unabashedly with it. '77 per cent Say No Solution Within Indian Constitution', the inaugural issue of *Outlook*[11] said on its cover. As expected, it triggered a backlash and Shiv Sainiks in Mumbai were provoked to attack the magazine's office in the city. If grabbing attention was the prime objective, Mehta did that with elan. *Outlook* got off to a dream beginning.

India Today responded quickly to the threat that the greenhorn posed. Within a few months, it turned from being a fortnightly into a weekly, reluctant to yield space to the rookie. The rivalry, though unstated, has continued in earnest to date. Having worked no less than twelve years with *India Today*, I took it seriously and had set up in my mind its journalistic standards as the minimum benchmark that I must surpass as the *Outlook* editor. I had tremendous respect and gratitude for the magazine, considered the Big Brother in the magazine genre for its reach and financial prowess that it now wielded as part of a group that has grown into a behemoth. Having once operated from a small, no-frills office in the inner circle of Delhi's Connaught Place opposite Palika Bazar, it now had graduated into a giant conglomerate, running popular 24/7 TV channels, a myriad of print publications and a string of web portals.

The size and scale of operations of the India Today group ought to have given me a complex, working for a smaller rival. Yet, I remained in awe of it, primarily because of my years in the magazine. I remained indebted to many of the editors who worked there and helped shape my career. In the 1990s, when I worked as an outstation *India Today* correspondent reporting from various states and neighbouring countries such as Bangladesh, the magazine was at its best. It invested huge amounts of money in its journalism and cut no corners in carrying out its craft. It commanded enormous respect, so much so that people considered it a sort of a Bible – the ultimate truth.

Back then, if something hadn't been reported in *India Today*, people didn't believe it entirely. Such people included my elder brother, whose opinion I value immensely. When I worked for the *Indian Express* for some years in the 1980s, I would excitedly show him what I had written for the paper. But a tough nut to crack, my brother would be less than moved. But *India Today* hasn't reported this, he would say, turning his incredulous gaze on me. It's a different matter that when, after a few years, I joined *India Today* as a correspondent, his opinion of the magazine changed. Ah! It seems the magazine's quality has declined, he said, pulling my leg.

Of course, I knew my brother was pleased with my progress. But he pretended and acted as the proverbial Big Brother, bullying the younger sibling a bit. I found in *India Today* a similar big brother to *Outlook*. The respect in which I held the magazine came from within. Among everything else, I held its owner and editor-in-chief, Aroon Purie, in great regard. The manner in which he ran editorial meetings and seemed to know more about a story than the most seasoned journalist on the beat was folklore. I watched him and wanted to emulate him if the opportunity ever came. And among the first things I did within hours of getting the appointment as *Outlook* editor was to write a personal email to Purie, seeking his blessings. Over the decades that he has helmed the group, Purie has seen hundreds of journalists come and go. But with me, he was exceptionally kind and responded immediately. He wished me well, though now I was in charge of a rival magazine.

So, as I set about doing better than *India Today* as the *Outlook* editor, I believe there was mutual respect. Yet, understandably, *India Today* wouldn't publicly acknowledge our existence. They pretended to be too big even to consider that we lurked somewhere close by. I, though, kept a close watch on it and was greatly amused to see that our rival intermittently chose to do the same cover stories a week or more after us. There were several such instances, including one on the stunning archaeological excavations in Rakhigarhi that shone new light on our ancient Harappan civilization. *Outlook* had scooped it and proudly put it on its cover in August 2018. A few weeks later, *India Today* did the same story and its editors boasted in online promo videos they were the first to have started work on the story. It didn't obviously matter that the story had already appeared in *Outlook*.

That *India Today* ignored *Outlook* – no matter what we did – as a matter of policy was a source of constant entertainment. My friends who still worked with *India Today* sometimes shared interesting snippets that I found extremely amusing. Apparently, every Monday, the top editors of *India Today* gather to review every magazine, comparing who did what and who did it better with the latest issue. It is obviously the right thing to do. But what did not seem right was how the review meetings invariably ended. Having gone through the contents of every magazine, the *India Today* editors reportedly concluded by saying *Outlook* has done this, *Week* has done that, but we have done the best. Then everyone applauded what had come to be a weekly ritual.

But I took *India Today* far more seriously, and when I saw its issue with 'The Failed State' cover, I hit the roof. Apart from the powerful image of the queued-up bodies on the cover, they had an exceptionally good issue. It opened with a very powerful editorial by Purie in which he didn't pull any punches against those in power. The rest of the cover was as powerful as it could get under the circumstances, with the magazine squarely putting the blame for the Covid-19 crisis that we all were being forced to live through, at the door of the government.

I knew I had to do something. And certainly, one better. Not that I needed any convincing about the dire circumstances during the second wave of the pandemic that was raging with the government conspicuous by its absence. I called for an emergency meeting of *Outlook*'s senior editorial staff that very evening, though we had only the previous day – Thursdays being the day when we normally decided on the next week's cover – agreed to go with a soft cover that we have been working on and which was reasonably cooked. Delhi was in the middle of a lockdown then, and my surprised editors joined me on a conference call in the evening, wondering what the urgency was all about. I told them about the change of plan: we were shelving next week's planned cover and going with a hard-hitting package on the government's mishandling of the Covid crisis instead. Let's pull it off, I said, throwing caution to the wind.

I often lamented that my *Outlook* editors were laid back, bordering on what could be perceived as laziness. They undoubtedly were a brilliant team with some great ideas and excellent skills. But what they lacked, I felt, was the killer instinct and that they didn't react proactively enough to changing news cycles. But notwithstanding this grouse, I knew they were a team that rallied wholeheartedly to the editor's call, and they responded enthusiastically to what I said. 'Absolutely!' 'Great idea!' They said in unison, and we immediately got down to work to pull off the next issue.

We didn't have the luxury of abundant time – we just had a few days – but the team was confident we could do it. Ideas were exchanged and several names were considered for columns that ideally should go into the issue. What about Pratap Bhanu Mehta? It would be fantastic if he agrees. How about Shashi Tharoor? He, too, is a strong name. As we discussed animatedly, the next issue began to take form. We wanted to take an incisive look at the performance of the Modi government with the Covid crisis as the immediate news peg. We must have a BJP voice as well, we agreed. Who could it be? We then zeroed in on Vijay Chauthaiwale, the head of the foreign affairs cell of the ruling party. We also quickly decided who among our reporters would report on what. The idea was to take a holistic view of the government's performance. It would be balanced, objective, even if it turned out to be unkind to the powers that be. The line-up of the content was drawn up in double-quick time.

I went to bed that night, somewhat content but with nagging bouts of concern. That there could be some costs for doing away with my customary caution did not elude me. I slept fitfully and, when I woke up, I contemplated what the future could hold. On top of my mind was how the magazine's owners would react. Then, how would the Modi government take it? Many in the media and the civil society had come to see the government as somewhat impatient with any form of criticism, and I, during my stint at *Hindustan Times*, had witnessed first-hand the abrupt ending of the editor-in-chief's tenure that is still spoken about highly for its no-nonsense professionalism.

Bobby Ghosh and I went back a long time, to our 1984 days in Vishakhapatnam. I was then in my first job and was posted in the seaside town of Andhra Pradesh for a brief while as the district correspondent of the now-defunct *Newstime* daily. We needed a stringer for our sports section, and we advertised for the position. Lots of applications were received, but the person we finally selected was Bobby. He was still in high school but showed promise. We offered him the job at a monthly wage of, if I remember correctly, Rs 200, and Bobby was off to a fascinating lifetime's journey in journalism.

I was in my early twenties and a lowly reporter at that time. But Bobby somehow saw me as his first boss, his mentor, and in later interviews he portrayed me as one of his earliest benefactors. According to him, I – a reporter with no more than Rs 700 as monthly salary but with a lot of attitude – had inspired him to take up journalism as a profession. I'm still not sure whether to be embarrassed or pleased about such fulsome praise. But that's a different story.

After a few months of working together in Vizag, which included leisurely strolls on its famed beach, with me puffing endless Charminar cigarettes – since I couldn't afford anything better – we parted ways and headed in different directions. Decades later, we met up again at the *Hindustan Times* headquarters in Delhi's Kasturba Gandhi Marg. By then, our roles had reversed. Having lived around the world and worked with *Time* and other prestigious publications and having made his name for his coverage of war-torn Iraq and other global hotspots, Bobby joined as the *HT* editor-in-chief. I was the paper's national affairs editor, running the paper's 100-plus team of reporters across the country.

We picked up from where we had left off. At his very first meeting with the senior *HT* staff, Bobby – true to his generous self – publicly announced that he was delighted to have joined a team that included his first boss. He doffed his hat towards me in public acknowledgement as I lowered my head, blushing in embarrassment. We worked and travelled together after that, though at times he got on my nerves, and I did not hide my displeasure. Having imbibed the gung-ho, no-nonsense Western style of journalism in adequate measure, Bobby brought in remarkable changes to *HT*'s reporting. There were no more holy cows, and there were suddenly no areas we couldn't report on.

It was too good to be true, and too good to last. Some months later – between June and August of 2017 – India and China were at loggerheads over Doklam, and *HT*'s coverage of the standoff apparently did not please officials who called the shots in the country. One day, a call reportedly came from someone very influential, requesting that a particular story be downplayed. Bobby heard him out but ignored his suggestion. The story was carried the next day with the prominence it deserved on the front page. Beginning then, Bobby was living on borrowed time. And when he pushed the envelope further by commissioning a 'Hate Tracker' – a section that catalogued hate crimes, such as the killing of Mohammed Akhlaq in Dadri over alleged possession of beef at home – we all suspected his time would be up soon. We were proven right. One day, Bobby suddenly announced he was leaving, triggering speculation about the reasons behind his sudden exit. They haven't died yet, despite the government and *HT* denying a report in The Wire which said that Bobby's departure was preceded by a meeting between the Prime Minister and the paper's owner. While the government denied as baseless the 'assumptions and insinuations' in the report, *HT* maintained Bobby had himself resigned.[12]

A company email couched in niceties hailed him as a great editor and contended that he had chosen to leave on his own. Yet, Bobby's departure weighed heavily on my mind as I slept fitfully that May night. 'Would I meet a similar end?' I wondered. I concluded that the issue critiquing the government's handling of the Covid crisis was the right thing to do. Thousands had been dropping dead, having contracted the virus, without oxygen and medical support. I told myself that staying silent at that point in time was nothing short of being complicit in mass murder.

Over the next few days, I confided in my wife and daughter my worries. Sitting across the dinner table, I played the devil's advocate, telling them what we were up to and what could happen. For one, I could be jobless. Two, they could even get a knock from government agencies – the income tax department, the department of revenue intelligence and what not. I told them whatever came to my mind – real or unreal – and they were horrified and worried. But hearing my argument, they came around. Always by my side, they were convinced of my logic and agreed that *Outlook* must speak up.

The editorial team worked at a frenetic pace all the while. Our senior editors and reporters got down to work in earnest. We intended to have a well-rounded look at the last seven years and Seema Guha, the foreign affairs editor, looked at India's – and particularly Prime Minister Modi's – international standing. What she finally went on to write wasn't exactly laudatory of the country's leadership. To the Western press, she argued, Modi was once the man who got things done. This larger-than-life image, she found, was in tatters – a fallout of Covid's second wave.[13] *Outlook*'s political editor, Bhavna Vij-Aurora, brought in all her experience to dissect the state of play in the government and the ruling party, apparently done in by the sudden onslaught of the second wave, which they had miserably failed to anticipate. To her, the Modi government suffered from the proverbial seven-year itch. Besides critics on the outside, even voices within the BJP were disquieted by the mishandling of the pandemic and Modi's style of functioning.

The team of crack reporters churned out more incisive pieces. Puneet Nicholas Yadav, a political reporter who wrote well, backed by solid understanding, turned his gaze on institutions – launched and designed with best intentions – that were increasingly falling prey to the trappings of what we knew as 'caged parrots'. What he wrote inspired little confidence. Our other reporters, Preetha Nair, Lola Nayar and Jyotika Sood, contributed in the making of the issue with their own reports – one more hard-hitting than the other. Luck seemed to be on our side with columnists that we approached, agreeing readily to write for the issue. The biggest catch was obviously Pratap Bhanu Mehta, undoubtedly the country's top public intellectual. Much in demand, Mehta had eluded us in the recent past, unable to find time amid his numerous commitments. But this time, he said yes. We knew instantly we had a winner on our hands.

As the columns came in, I sat down to write my own editorial. What I ended up writing was perhaps the most caustic of columns I had written to date. Adequately angry and upset with what we had been experiencing at the peak of the health crisis, the words came easy. And the sentences they helped string together was a full-throated condemnation of our political class. I didn't mention any politician by name in my editorial. But I left nothing to the imagination as to who I was addressing. Having argued that our leaders had failed us terribly, I wound it up thus: 'We cowered as a consequence, but the leaders also stood uncovered in our eyes. Rather than being tall and towering with wide protective chests, they turned out to be small and weak when the real test came.'[14]

However uncharitable, my editorial was nothing in comparison to the essay written by Pratap Bhanu Mehta, an unparalleled wordsmith with unique clarity of thought. Titled 'The Empire of Cruelty',[15] Mehta tore into the Modi government like no one possibly could:

> Modi's political success was his ability to produce an identification with himself. Partly this was a story rooted in biography, where his personal rise was itself seen as a rebuke to an old plutocratic, dynastic order. Partly this was produced by growing Hindu communalism; his ability to project himself as the personification of Hindus. In his telling, he is their political saviour, their high priest, who symbolically liberated them from a thousand-year subjugation and seeming pusillanimity, and gave them the strength to assert ruthless political power. This is the avatar he took on in what he might perhaps consider the high point of his seven years: the bhoomi pujan of the mandir at Ayodhya. Part of it was produced by an unmediated communication style, a claim of being able to intuit what the people want. Perhaps, communication is a misnomer here, since the style involves no listening. It is rather a claim to an intuitive identification.

Mehta's column then went on to detail why he believed Modi had transformed cruelty into an art form, arguing that many in the country saw it as a show of strength. The rich wanted Modi to curb and discipline populist demands. The less privileged wished Modi to smash old power structures and dismantle the elite. All in all, a vast majority of the country wanted Modi to exercise ruthless power.

Para by para, Mehta dismantled Modi's aura as a benevolent ruler. By the time he concluded his column, he had stripped the government of its greatest showpiece. 'This regime's greatest achievement in seven years is that it made us a nation of resentful hearts, small minds and constricted souls. We might think this is a failure. But this is how the Modi-government set out to define its success, and it succeeded all too well,' Mehta said, in summing up his column.

From where Mehta ended, Shashi Tharoor – the immensely articulate Congress parliamentarian from Kerala with a penchant for using long-winded, little-used words – took off. In the column that he wrote from his hospital bed while he battled a bout of Covid, Tharoor came up with a veritable charge sheet of the government. 'How did everything go so wrong so soon after India was being described around the world as a success story, having recovered from the "first wave" last year, resumed normal life and economic activity, and started exporting vaccines? The list of errors is indeed long.'

The list of politicians we had lined up for the magazine issue allowed no let-up for a government that was, for many of us, nowhere to be found when we needed it the most. Mahua Moitra, the acerbic Trinamool Congress MP who had made a name for herself by repeatedly stealing the show on the floor of the Lok Sabha with her fiery speeches, was travelling. But she agreed to be interviewed and said things true to herself. 'Modi brought India to its knees', she said. Not to be outdone, RJD MP Manoj Kumar Jha pulled no punches in his column. 'The pandemic is moving into a hinterland that has already been made barren by an uncaring government,' he contended, citing the bodies that floated on the Ganga to our horror.

It was a macabre story that screamed all along for us to speak up and take a stand. Yet, we did not lose sight of the fact that we ought to give space to those who supported the government. It was in our DNA to listen to all sides – however far-fetched and disagreeable – and we readily provided a platform to Vijay Chauthaiwale, head of the BJP's foreign affairs cell. Chauthaiwale had been more than an acquaintance. At a time when Modi had spoken out against his critics whom he derisively described as the 'Khan Market Gang'[16] – named after the seemingly left liberal's favourite haunt, dotted with pubs and cafes in a plush Delhi neighbourhood – I had encouraged Chauthaiwale to write his take on Khan Market. In his article that we published prominently as the 'Khan Market Diary', Chauthaiwale had held forth on what he perceived were the many wrongs of those who hung around the place. Though I frequented it often, I had a hearty laugh. And I and Chauthaiwale routinely joked that we must meet up to have lunch together – of all places, at Khan Market.

Chauthaiwale did not disappoint this time, too, though I must say he didn't have much of an idea what our issue would turn out to be. We also didn't tell him. 'Those who keep dreaming of dislodging Narendra Modi from power have no idea of his single-minded focus on serving the people, and the goodwill he generates from it,' he held forth in defence of the discredited government in his column. We had no qualms in publishing it.

With the columns in place and the deadline fast approaching, it was time now to turn our focus on the cover. Ideas were exchanged and debated. I still felt that it wasn't necessary to put the image of Modi or Shah on the cover. We could make the point without having to, I opined. Then a brainwave struck. 'How about making it look like a police 'missing' poster?' asked Sunil Menon, one of my deputies. We jumped at the idea. Our resident design chief, Deepak Sharma, went to work, and the cover that turned out to be the most controversial in recent history began taking shape.

I always had immense faith in my editorial team, and if I needed any further reiteration, the late-night discussions we had on the phone sealed it. Deepak came up with the cover. 'Missing' it proclaimed in red against a white background with a minimalist black border. Underneath, it had three staccato lines.

Name: Government of India.
Age: 7 years.
Inform: Citizens of India.

The cover summed up what we wanted to say, and it went to press. Then followed the various columns and reports in phases. By the time the job was entirely done by the editorial staff in the early hours of Thursday, I was fast asleep. I woke up to tweet the cover and brace myself for the response.

What followed was a deluge. I guessed a lot was happening but had no clue what. Apart from Dharmendra, no BJP leader got in touch with me directly. Some – though not exactly occupying positions of power but somewhat aligned with the system – made discreet inquiries as to what was inside. The magazine had not hit the stands yet, and it would not till the next day when it would also be available online. All that people could do was guess.

I, too, wondered what the consequences could be, pacing up and down the narrow balcony of our home. I got the first hint when afternoon gave way to dusk and darkness enveloped Delhi in the middle of a lockdown. *Outlook* CEO Indranil Roy called, sounding nervous and shaken. As the practice has always been, I had kept him informed of the issue, and he knew about the 'Missing' cover. And that morning, when one of the owners asked what the cover was, he had told them about it. Both found it funny – that there was a cover notifying the government to be missing – and they shrugged it off with a laugh. The banter lasted only till the evening, though, when the fireworks started.

Indranil sounded panic-stricken. Apparently, there were incessant calls from Mumbai demanding answers about the cover. He was also asked for details of the articles in the issue. The management was reportedly very stressed. With tempers clearly frayed, Indranil's nervousness grew. He called me every half hour, relaying what he was being told. No less tense than him, I listened. But I volunteered a way out. 'If it's getting too difficult to handle, tell them I am willing to step down,' I suggested. A long-time acquaintance – I had known him since my *India Today* days in Kolkata, when he was a circulation executive who would often sit on the floor to tie up bundles of the magazine – Indranil shut me up. 'Now you stop making it worse,' he said, hanging up only to call back at ever shorter intervals.

I wasn't directly in the line of fire, yet. Unlike many other media owners, *Outlook*'s promoters seemed to have a different set of principles. They generally kept away from the editor and editorial matters, and in the three years that I had been associated with *Outlook*, they would have spoken to me no more than six times – that too mostly to understand the hidden nuances of something that had happened, such as the accusations by the Mumbai police commissioner Param Bir Singh in early 2021 that he had been asked to collect bribes by the Maharashtra home minister. But for setting a kind of a red line the day I had been appointed editor, they had never dictated *Outlook*'s editorial line. I thrived under their non-interference, telling anyone and everyone who cared to listen that I must be one of the luckiest editors in the country, allowed to do what was required to be done.

And then the call from Mumbai finally came. It was past nine when they decided to speak to me, but I must clarify for the sake of record that there was no sign of rancour in their voices. Speaking to the editor, they were respectful. 'Our phones have not stopped ringing. We are under pressure that we cannot handle,' Akshay – one of Rajan Raheja's two sons – said. I, too, explained why I had chosen to do the cover – not doing it would have been complicit in mass deaths – and he heard me out. 'I understand. But you now keep quiet. Don't do anything,' Akshay suggested.

I readily agreed – having already done what I had to do. Basically, the Rahejas were asking me not to stir up any more trouble while they were firefighting. 'Will you lie low, please?' asked Akshay. I said I had no problem.

As I understood, the phones of the Rahejas had not stopped ringing since the evening when the news of the 'Missing' cover had reached those who mattered the most. They then faced non-stop demands: from pulping the entire print edition to killing the issue online. The first was out of the question as copies had already reached many destinations. Now, discussions veered around to how to minimise the damage online.

After my conversation with Akshay, I was again out of the loop. Two hours later, I got a call from the office, and a new cover was sent on my mobile for my clearance. This didn't mention 'Missing', but instead had mugshots of the contributors – Pratap Bhanu Mehta, Shashi Tharoor, Manoj Kumar Jha and others – with the caption

'Read in this Issue'. The rest looked like our regular covers: it had the *Outlook* masthead with price and date. I put my foot down. Nothing doing, I said, insisting the cover could not be changed. I wonder what would have happened had I capitulated and agreed. My credibility would have been ruined forever. But fortunately, I was still in my senses and able to think clearly. More calls followed, and I gradually understood what was being worked out. The idea was to minimise the damage by hiding the controversial cover when the issue was uploaded online the next day.

A compromise was worked out overnight. Though I held my ground that the cover of the print magazine would not be changed, I agreed that a promo with mugshots of all the authors could be uploaded to introduce the issue online, instead of the customary print cover. But it wouldn't exactly be the cover and would not have the customary *Outlook* masthead. I was willing to yield a little and allow the management some wriggle room to make peace with whoever they wanted to placate.

It was, however, easier said than done. The moment the issue went online with the promo instead of the cover, people, led by TMC MP Mahua Moitra, called our bluff. She tweeted, pointing out that the 'Missing' cover was not to be seen anywhere on the *Outlook* website and launched a tirade, attacking the owners. 'So Outlookindia latest cover had Missing Govt of India on advertised online cover. Pushback from govt made them change online cover. Come on Raheja group – give up publishing if you can't stick to your stand!', she wrote.[17]

She was both right and wrong. Yes, there was an attempted cover-up – to minimise the damage – but it was not true that we had changed the cover. I had shot down the idea the previous night. So, Moitra's tweet went viral even as my original tweet announcing the 'Missing' cover did the rounds even more furiously than before. Moitra's tweet now ignited a new controversy, with people beginning to question our integrity. Having pledged my silence, I kept quiet. But an agitated Sunil Menon, *Outlook*'s managing editor and my deputy, called to question me as to why I had capitulated. He knew nothing about what had transpired through the previous evening, and he had fallen for what Moitra claimed: that we had changed the cover.

I explained myself to Sunil. Is it the cover? Where is the *Outlook* masthead? The date, price, etc.? I took him through all that had happened and assured him that I had actually stopped a new cover from being made. Sunil was convinced. Can I go on Twitter and explain the facts, he asked? I said go ahead, and Sunil took to Twitter. But to little avail. The promo – minus the masthead – had been mistaken for the cover, and we continued to get pasted on social media even as heaps of praise came our way for the issue. A spat ensued between Sunil and Moitra, who refused to back down from her assertion that we had changed the cover. She had a point. Our original cover was not to be found online, and then other journalists got in on the act. They began calling me to ask why the 'Missing' cover had gone missing. Told to lie low, I ducked all questions. It added to the intrigue, and several websites went ahead to report that *Outlook*'s much talked about cover was controversially missing.

We belatedly realized that we were playing the game badly. Not having the cover online was an own goal. I called Indranil again. Better sense prevailed, and a way was found. Instead of just the promo, we now created a GIF that had both the promo and the 'Missing' cover. Being a GIF, it rotated the two images: when one came to the homepage of the *Outlook* website, one saw first the promo – for about 10 seconds – and then the missing cover for some three seconds. The controversial cover was hidden, but not entirely.

The cover, however, continued to make waves – both nationally and internationally. The latest *Outlook* issue was seen as signs of the Indian media finally finding its voice that many felt had been suppressed and silenced. From Australia to Turkey, the media took note and wrote about *Outlook*. Even CNN reached out and reported on what we had done. Having laid low for some time, I treaded cautiously and took care not to sound pompous. 'What we did was not an act of bravery. We were just being objective,' I was quoted by CNN, explaining that there was indeed a sense of having been abandoned in the country in the wake of the second surge of Covid-19.

But my careful explanations did little to put the lid on the uproar that our cover had stoked. It remained a hot topic that got heated further a few days later, with the BJP top brass alleging that it was part of a Congress toolkit. Led by the likes of BJP spokesman Sambit Patra, the party released what it said was an elaborate plan by the opposition Congress to sully the image of the government.[18] Among the many things it alleged, it said magazines had been told to use the word 'missing' wherever the opportunity arose to portray the government in bad light. The Congress denied the charge and FIRs were lodged against several BJP functionaries[19] for cooking up fictitious charges. As the BJP and the Congress locked horns, Twitter stepped in to brand the tweets of the BJP functionaries as 'manipulated'.[20] It meant the allegations they made were dubious in nature. The BJP saw red, and the Delhi police visited the Twitter headquarters. As with everything else, the controversy now took a political colour.

Holed up in my home, I knew that the accusation that the word 'missing' was used to discredit the government under instructions from an opposition party was blatantly wrong. It had no basis. When we first ideated the issue, 'missing' was not on our minds. The idea hit us when we worked on the cover, and it was entirely ours – the four or five of us who were on the editorial team. Yet, the allegation and the subsequent controversy cast their shadow. A very prominent Union minister messaged one of my editors, citing the toolkit claim and saying that I was amenable to the Congress. Even some in the *Outlook* management were swayed. They discreetly inquired how close I was to the opposition party. Is Ruben really close to the Congress? Does he really take orders from the party, they asked. In no time, the 'Missing' cover assumed an ominous portent of making or unmaking me.

2

50 CRORES VERSUS 50,000 CRORES

OUR CIVILIZATIONAL CALENDAR IS DIVIDED INTO TWO DISTINCT phases – BCE (Before the Common Era) and CE (Common Era). That's what they are currently called as opposed to the earlier practice of describing them as BC (Before Christ) and AD (Anno Domini) which, because of references to Christ, weren't considered secular enough. Whatever be the case, my stint as *Outlook*'s editor can also be lumped into two different segments – PM and AM, pre-Missing and after-Missing.

The first three years at *Outlook* had been a breeze – challenging, eventful, but extremely satisfying. The challenges that awaited me from the first day of my editorship were many – from the mundane task of finding my way to the magazine's Delhi office in one corner of a crowded market complex in Safdarjung Enclave – made more famous by the succulent kebabs available at the Rajinder Da Dhaba – to finding acceptance in a team many of whom had spent years in the organization and were wary of me. Though I used to visit Delhi on short official trips earlier, I had never lived in the city. I came to live here only after I returned to India from my long stint in West Asia, and I was yet to discover Delhi fully when I reported for duty at *Outlook* in June 2018. And in doing so, I got lost.

It isn't that I had not visited *Outlook*'s office before. A friend had worked there many years ago and I had accompanied him to work once or twice. I had also visited while looking for a job just before returning to the country. But on all those occasions, I was driven to the place. Also, my interviews before I became the editor were never at the *Outlook* office. They happened at cafes and then in the corporate office of the Rahejas in Mumbai. So, the day I was supposed to join, I took a cab and got down before Rajinder Da Dhaba. Then I went around sweating for quite some time, unable to locate the exact office.

Once inside, I was more sure-footed. Winning over the trust of the editorial team wasn't difficult. They required transparency, and I was able to offer them that. As things fell into place, we began doing some great work together. Apart from the quality of the editorial team I had, the biggest asset that I undoubtedly inherited was *Outlook*'s legacy. Founded in 1995, the magazine was synonymous with its founding editor, Vinod Mehta, and that gave it instant recognition and acceptance. I recognized *Outlook*'s inherent strength and attempted to build on it further, rather than trying to make my own mark by denying its stellar past.

I was looking to make a statement, and the first thing I did on occupying what was once Mehta's office was to get a photograph of his framed and hang it on the wall behind me. It was strange that the office had no photographs or memorabilia of Vinod Mehta – *Outlook*'s biggest source of public goodwill. At an *Outlook* event attended by Union ministers and a roomful of VIPs soon after, I spoke about how Mehta – the legendary editor – keeps an eye on me from behind my back. Though I had never had the opportunity to work with him – having only seen Mehta once from a distance and, of course, having read all his engrossing columns and books – the respect for him came naturally to me. The showmanship that I indulged in possibly had a touch of design, though.

I also revelled in the fact that none interfered with my work. The CEO, Indranil Roy, had been a long-time acquaintance and we seemed to be natural allies. We worked in tandem while the promoters, ensconced in their impregnable tower in Mumbai, stayed away. For the first three years, they rarely called and perhaps had little idea about what we were up to. Most of the time, they had no advance information on what the *Outlook* covers would be, finding out only when the issues reached them. This was a marked departure from my days at *Hindustan Times*, where a call came every evening to the news desk from the second floor, enquiring about the line-up of the next day's front page. The very mention of the country's top politician in a headline led to further queries and often caused grief. Just the way it once did while I drove back home. My phone rang as I drove past a police barricade at Lajpat Nagar, and I was quizzed about a rather innocuous story that had 'Modi' in the headline. I had no problem explaining the story, but the traffic cops on duty were less understanding. They fined me for talking on the mobile while driving.

Once at *Outlook*, I considered myself one of the luckiest editors in the country with zero interference. The first three years flew by with the management treating me with what I understood as respect. Even when they did call – like when a reporter stumbled upon a story about a minister, son of a powerful southern state chief minister, using a chartered plane to fly to Davos – they resisted issuing any diktats. They simply enquired what the story was about. Not that I knew about the minister-son's foreign jaunt when the first call came. The reporter had come across it through his sources and had not intimated me at the time.

'Hey Ruben, are we breaking a big story about a southern state', I was rather startled to be asked out of the blue. 'What story', I replied, mystified. 'No, no … there is a big story happening. The chief minister's office has called.' Still clueless, I didn't have an answer. As I wondered what the matter was, more calls came, and this time I was told the reporter's name. 'He is the one doing the story.' I called the reporter to check. 'Arrey Sir, I am checking right now. Story *toh abhi banaa nahi* (I haven't written the story yet),' he said, apologetic for not keeping me in the loop.

The pieces fell in place thereafter, and the mystery was unravelled. The reporter had been tipped off that the son had gone to attend the global financial summit in Switzerland's Davos, but unlike other Union ministers and dignitaries who had flown economy class on commercial airlines, he and a group of five others had first flown to Gujarat and then by a chartered private aircraft to Davos. But more significantly, the aircraft was hired by a real estate firm with business interests in the state ruled by the minister-son's father. Brought to his notice, the reporter got in touch with the chief minister's office. They panicked and reportedly called up the minister-son, who at that point was about to return. The chartered plane was, in fact, taxiing on the runway when the passengers were alerted to the *Outlook* reporter's query. The plane aborted its take-off, went back to the terminal and the group quickly disembarked and took a regular flight back home. The chief minister's office now wanted the story spiked.

I informed the Rahejas of the facts in my possession. They had been calling incessantly, but to their credit they did not ask me to kill the story. It was obvious, though, that the story would inconvenience them as they were into real estate as well. It's a different matter that the story finally did not materialise. We needed more supporting documents, which the reporter's source promised but eventually did not deliver. He got scared, saving us the dilemma of whether to carry or kill the story.

For all practical purposes, the *Outlook* management lived up to the principle of not meddling with matters pertaining to editorial. The family patriarch, Rajan Raheja, never called. The sons called but rarely, only to exchange notes on significant developments for the purpose of figuring out whether I had some extra information or gossip to go with. The conversations mostly stayed light-hearted and were never serious.

It did turn serious, to my dismay, within two months of our controversial 'Missing' cover.

Mindful of my own future, I thought I was being clever when I quickly changed gears in an attempt to tone down the uproar we had triggered. Having made a statement – loud and clear – with the 'Missing' cover, the following week, we turned our gaze on the centenary of the film maestro Satyajit Ray. It was an eclectic cover package[1] that sold well. And why not? The issue was of a kind that one would like to collect and keep for good. Shining a light on the life and times of Ray across the pages of *Outlook* that week were some of those who knew and understood his art intimately and were also involved in his creative journey – Sharmila Tagore being one of them. Dhritiman Chatterjee, who began his acting career as the protagonist of Ray's *Pratidwandi* in 1970 and essayed another important role in the maestro's acclaimed movie *Ganashatru* some twenty years later, was another top name writing in the issue.

For me, it was business as usual. After Ray, came a cover on the journey of the Covid vaccine – by road, air and boats across the length and breadth of the country[2] at a time when vaccination appeared to be sluggish and the challenge of providing timely jabs to a billion-plus population seemed daunting. As always, *Outlook* continued to chart a distinctive course that we believed would set us apart from the rest. In the coming weeks, we ran a cover – among everything else – on the phenomenon of Malayalam movies growing increasingly popular on OTT platforms. We called it 'Cinema*layalam*'.

Just when I thought everything had settled back to normal, I was in for a rude awakening. It was about the time when Jesuit priest Stan Swamy died in judicial custody,[3] and the country was caught up in a renewed debate over its controversial terror laws. Such laws – Unlawful Activities (Prevention) Act (UAPA) and Section 124A of the Indian Penal Code dealing with sedition included – had been in the news for quite some time for what had come to be seen as their indiscriminate misuse, but perhaps never as intensely as in the aftermath of Swamy's death.

Against the backdrop of a state that seemingly was intolerant of dissent and allegedly determined to shut down critics, it seemed that the laws were being flagrantly abused to lock up anyone opposed to the government. There was abundant evidence of this – from the jailing of Dr Kafeel Khan,[4] who blew the whistle on children's deaths in Gorakhpur in Uttar Pradesh during a particularly bad epidemic, to the detention of a journalist on the way to Hathras in the days following the horrific death of a Dalit girl allegedly raped and assaulted by a group of upper caste boys.[5] Anyone who said anything or seemed to be acting against the establishment was being ensnared by the stringent laws and thrown behind bars. The country was awash with brazen instances of injustice. Several cartoonists and stand-up comics had been punished as well. Several activists were in jail over what on the face of it seemed to be their rather tenuous roles in the riots that rocked the nation's capital in early 2020.[6]

The misuse of anti-terror laws[7] had since long been a point of divisive debate, and the death of the octogenarian Swamy added fuel to it. The soft-spoken activist who had spent his lifetime taking up just causes of poor and exploited tribals in the most under-developed parts of the country found himself in jail over what has come to be known as the infamous 'Bhima Koregaon case'. He was yet another of a dozen-odd people – activists, academics and lawyers – thrown behind bars with little chance of getting bail as first the police in Pune and then the NIA investigated an alleged plot in the aftermath of a violent protest in the small Maharashtra town some 25 km from Pune.

Described as the 'Elgar Parishad' to commemorate the historical victory of Dalits in the Battle of Bhima Koregaon, people from across the country had gathered, as they had been doing every year, when violence broke out in 2018, resulting in one death. It is alleged that people from the upper castes attacked the congregation, but subsequent police investigations took a different course. It was alleged that prominent persons behind the event had plotted to create trouble, including against the state. It was further alleged that they had even been planning to assassinate the Prime Minister.

The plot – largely unsubstantiated to date – thickened, and prominent intellectuals found themselves charged under the most draconian laws, and jailed. Sudha Bharadwaj, Rona Wilson, Varavara Rao, Anand Teltumbde – the list grew longer as indignation over what many saw as 'brazen overreach' by the establishment also grew proportionately. Over subsequent months and years, the case built by the state seemed increasingly weak amid allegations of evidence tampering. Independent probes hinted at computers of many of the accused being hacked and evidence planted.[8] But the laws under which they had been charged were such that a majority of the accused got no succour. They stayed in jail.

Swamy, arrested in October 2020 and lodged in a Maharashtra jail, met a worse fate. A patient of Parkinson's disease, his health deteriorated without adequate medical help. The authorities made it even more difficult, rejecting his initial requests for a straw and sipper cup to drink from. Even as Swamy struggled to carry out his daily chores, he contracted Covid. As he grew weaker and struggled to speak coherently, his lawyers knocked on the doors of the courts for an early bail on medical grounds. But the proceedings dragged on, and when finally, a court convened to hear his latest petition, news came that Swamy had passed away.

The news caused outrage, both nationally and internationally. It was a story *Outlook* could not ignore. Soon after, the country's chief justice, N.V. Ramana,[9] spoke out publicly, voicing popular sentiment. He dubbed the misuse of sedition laws as a 'serious breach of functioning of institutions' and asked the Central government to explain why it still retained the colonial-era legislation in the statute books when it had done away with so many other archaic laws. Another Supreme Court judge, D.Y. Chandrachud, spoke out in a similar vein around the same time.[10]

The anti-sedition law and terror laws such as the UAPA were clearly in the spotlight, and we at *Outlook* got down to work. It called for nothing less than a cover, we agreed. But never to tread the beaten track, we began to put together an exhaustive package on how the laws were being misused by almost everyone across the country. It wasn't just the BJP on whose watch Swamy was jailed and died. The rot was more extensive and entrenched and prevailed across states ruled by other political parties too.

As our reporters began documenting the abuse of laws in their respective territories, I was convinced that our approach was objective and balanced. We weren't putting the BJP alone in the dock. Instead, we were being even-handed and critical of all political parties including Mamata Banerjee's Trinamool Congress, K. Chandrashekar Rao's Telangana Rashtra Samithi (TRS) and Naveen Patnaik's Biju Janata Dal (BJD).

Rather than being circumspect, I was confident that the cover we worked on would be powerful and in the public interest. I finished writing an editorial that was to serve as an opener, which purposefully portrayed our powerful politicians in poor light. It began like this:

> Father Stan Swamy did not die alone earlier this month. Irony died alongside too as several opposition leaders – always quick to score a political point – came together shortly afterwards to sign a letter to the country's President, complaining about the injustice done to the jailed tribal rights campaigner, and the 'draconian' nature of the Unlawful Activities (Prevention) Act (UAPA), the anti-terrorism law the authorities used to arrest him. A lot has been said and written since Swamy's death, and none in the right frame of mind can justify the sad circumstances that engulfed his final hours and days. The

> motley group of opposition leaders was right in highlighting the travesty. But where many of them went wrong was that they did not turn the spotlight on themselves and left many things unanswered.[11]

While never losing sight of the fact that Swamy had died on the BJP's watch, I went on to catalogue the dubious role of other parties during their stints in power. 'For all practical purposes, the misuse of terror laws is not a problem of a particular political party. If Swamy had to pay the price … many more have had their lives turned upside down under others as well, for instance, the Congress, the Trinamool Congress, and the Communists', I argued. I was particularly harsh on P. Chidambaram, the Congress leader who had also been the Union home minister between 2008 and 2012. I contended that Chidambaram, who now preaches morality from his perch as a newspaper columnist, had waxed eloquent on how and why locking up people without easy access to bail had its virtues when the UAPA was amended and given more teeth during his tenure.

I was comforted by the fact that the package was coming together exactly the way we planned it. Legal expert Faizan Mustafa had sent in a powerful piece[12] documenting in detail the historical and geographical spread of the misuse of the laws. 'Harsher laws have always been used to suppress dissent and political opposition', he wrote. Our own reporters worked to document what was left unsaid. In Mamata Banerjee's Bengal, activists had been booked under UAPA for protesting against a power project, reported our Kolkata correspondent, Snigdhendu Bhattacharya. Sandeep Sahu, reporting from Odisha ruled by Naveen Patnaik, shone light on how the draconian laws had been invoked to jail critics.[13] Altogether, they made for a rather unsavoury reading.

With the package ready to roll with the cover title 'The Tyranny of Terror Laws', another big story broke that prompted us to ponder our cover choice. The Pegasus story forced many to wonder whether we had turned into a surveillance state. It made waves across the globe, with a consortium of media houses coming together for what they claimed was one of the biggest exposes of recent times. According to them, governments of many countries, India included, had deployed an Israeli spyware to mount surveillance on people they were interested in. In India, people reportedly spied on by infecting their mobile phones with the spyware included several ministers, journalists and the Congress leader Rahul Gandhi.[14]

Because of the nature of the controversy and the gravity of the charges, the story was headline news everywhere. For days on end, Pegasus was the most searched word on Google and on top of everyone's mind. The government's reluctance to deny it categorically – if any of its arms had actually acquired and deployed the spyware legally or illegally – deepened the controversy further. For a while, we at *Outlook* were also tempted to consider the Pegasus story as a potential cover. Then I decided against it. In my considered view, Pegasus was a story wholly owned by the consortium of media houses that had unearthed it. They reported details in dribs and drabs – adding more names to the ones suspected to have been spied on – and we realized we would not be throwing any spectacular new light on the controversy. We could only report what the consortium had already reported on and, at best, provide context alongside the background.

Given that our credo was to be consistently different, I ultimately took the call that we would go with the 'Tyranny of Terror Laws' as our cover while exhaustively reporting on the Pegasus controversy for the purpose of keeping our readers well informed. So, Pegasus found a mention in our next week's cover – on the top above the *Outlook* masthead as the second most important story in the issue – while the focus firmly stayed on our extensive and exclusive reportage on terror laws. I was convinced that our well-rounded and balanced coverage on both the abuse of terror laws and the Pegasus controversy would enhance our credibility as a fair and objective magazine.

As with the terror law coverage, our Pegasus coverage didn't lose sight of neutrality. We traced the history of alleged spying on political opponents in the country and attempted to put the current controversy in the right context. Was such surveillance – authorised or unauthorised – possible? We allowed a wide range of experts to have their say. 'If you believe your phone's not been hacked, you are living in a fool's paradise', argued former Union home secretary Gopal Krishna Pillai in an interview with *Outlook*'s political editor Bhavna Vij-Aurora. Others held forth on the issue that was to snowball into a major debate in the absence of a categorical denial by the Central government. Though it was unclear if people at large understood its significance, opposition parties were on the warpath over it. With the government dragging its feet and reluctant to engage, the subsequent parliament session was a washout with any constructive debate lost in the din.

Outlook held its ground while reporting on Pegasus. As always, we provided space to divergent views and one columnist, Jaijit Bhattacharya – a tech expert – argued that while such surveillance was eminently possible, it was also in the realm of possibility that such an act was carried out by someone else, not necessarily the government of the day. Bhattacharya wrote:

> Others who could possibly gain from such widespread surveillance are key opposition politicians themselves. We do have savvy politicians from various parts of the country such as Maharashtra and Uttar Pradesh who do harbour ambitions of being the Prime Minister and they do stand to gain from tapping into the phones of the said targets. However, as per NSO – the Israeli manufacturer of the spyware – they sell it only to governments. So does that rule out non-governmental players? Or does it? Pegasus has been known to have been used by Mexican drug cartels to target and to intimidate journalists and government actors. So clearly the spyware has now moved into the hands of non-state actors. So it could potentially be the opposition politicians also who could be the perpetrators of the surveillance.[15]

What Bhattacharya argued evidently gave an escape route to the embattled government, and at least some members of the editorial team found it far-fetched. They objected and said we shouldn't be sticking our neck out by giving it a platform. But sworn to objectivity and all-sides opinion, I found it interesting. Why not? Let's carry it, I decreed, and Bhattacharya's column appeared, shedding light on something that many found politically inconvenient and possibly, incorrect. The issue out of the printing press, I felt we had done a good job presenting varied and even conflicting views.

But if I had hopes of floating in cloud nine for some time, I was in for a disappointment. Unlike other weeks when non-editorial staff routinely complimented me for bringing out a good issue, this time, it was markedly different. That something was not right was evident from Indranil's long face the moment he came into my room. He looked visibly shaken. What he told me stunned me. Apparently, he had received a call, and the management wasn't happy at all with our latest issue. The details narrated thereafter left me speechless. It was conveyed to me that we shouldn't have done either of the two stories – the one on terror laws and the other on Pegasus. Hearing him, I held my head in grief.

Though not exactly alarmed, what I heard confused me. That I didn't instantly hit the panic button was primarily because I had immense faith in the work I had done for the past three years. For most of that period, the management kept a distance and I interpreted it to be a sign of their confidence that I enjoyed. I also saw it – albeit mistakenly – as a mark of respect for the editor. But the conversation with the CEO that afternoon unmistakably sowed the seeds of confusion. Various thoughts crossed my mind, but the one that weighed in the most was – what was *Outlook*, after all. Positioned as a news magazine – one of the country's foremost – its proud tagline proclaimed, 'the fully loaded magazine'. It meant we reported news without fear or favour and without prejudices.

The latest issue was no different. For the package on terror laws, we had been as forthright as possible, showing the mirror to all political parties that were to be blamed for their misuse. For that matter, our matter-of-fact reporting could be used by the BJP to deflect criticism. Though we clearly blamed the party for its constant abuse of the laws, they could also cite our coverage to lay the blame on others – other political parties in power in other parts of the country and in different periods – for repeated and more frequent violations. Ditto with our Pegasus coverage. At a time when the media was overwhelmingly focused on blaming the Central government, we did raise the possibility of the spyware being stealthily deployed by others as well. While underlining that such surveillance was entirely possible given the technological advancements, we did add – even at the cost of appearing politically incorrect – that the misuse could even have been ordered by some opposition politicians. Coverage of the issue could not possibly have been more objective than *Outlook*'s.

I attempted to defend our choice of stories, but the CEO didn't seem to be convinced. After a while, he stopped listening. He didn't categorically say we were wrong. But he didn't say we were right either. He kept conveying the message that we should be staying clear of controversial stories. I was given to understand that our terror law story had shown the BJP in poor light. It didn't matter that we had focused on other political parties as well. Same apparently was the case with the Pegasus story, which supposedly added to the ruling party's embarrassment. My defence failed to cut any ice.

The conversation was happening around the time when sections of the media in the country were under increased scrutiny by the powers that be, and *Dainik Bhaskar* – a prominent newspaper chain with massive circulation in the Hindi heartland – had just been raided by the income tax department.[16] *Bhaskar* had a chequered history, but its journalism in the recent past – particularly during the Covid second wave – had been praiseworthy. For some inexplicable reason, the media house had turned very critical of the Union government and its reporters scoured the countryside to document tales of death and despair wrought by the pandemic and worsened by the alleged inept handling of the crisis by an unprepared establishment.[17] From unaccounted bodies floating in the Ganga to the dead being given undignified burials on the riverbanks – *Bhaskar* worked hard to expose the true extent of the human catastrophe unfolding at the time. The newspaper chain also reported what many of us suspected: that the actual death count from Covid during the second surge was much higher than what official figures suggested.[18] Its reporters went from one crematorium to another to document deaths that simply were not being taken into account by the officialdom.

Then the income tax officials came calling, raiding *Bhaskar*'s owners and editors. This was not the first time that a media house was being subjected to what was perceived to be a crackdown meant to stifle its voice. A few months earlier, in February 2021, NewsClick – a news web portal – had been subjected to similar treatment, with raids on its premises lasting days. Its offices were visited by income tax officials again some months later for what was supposed to be 'surveys'. The government said the raids were legitimate and they were only acting on credible information about financial violations.[19] Its critics were not convinced, but the cumulative effect of the raids was chilling.

Hearing my CEO caution me about the content that we could or could not produce, I couldn't help wondering if the *Bhaskar* raids had anything to do with it. Certainly, surprised by its suddenness, I sought clarity. 'If we are a news magazine, then how is it that we won't cover news? And if we are not to cover, what are we meant to do?' I asked. With no clear answers forthcoming from the CEO, I continued: 'Are we ceasing to be a news magazine? What are we then – a lifestyle magazine, or a magazine devoted entirely to fashion or culture?'

My point was simple: I needed clarity. I wasn't willing to compromise on journalistic ethics. While exercising caution that we had grown accustomed to doing, I wasn't prepared to give up wholly on our news coverage. While not being rabidly anti-government, I wasn't willing to dramatically swing to the other extreme either, ignoring totally what the powers that be wished to be whitewashed.

The CEO promised to get back in a couple of days and provide me with clarity. It never came. Instead, things began to unravel quickly, with administrative issues that had been bubbling in the background suddenly coming to the forefront. These included cost-cutting in our editorial operations. Bringing down costs – salary expenses in particular – had always been a contentious issue at *Outlook*, with pressure mounting to let go of people not seen as essential for our operations. Revenues had been shrinking over the years – accentuated further by the economic slowdown brought on by the pandemic – and the financial situation had turned dire. What started as salary delays for a few weeks had spilled into months – by as much as five months at the height of the pandemic – and I concurred with the management that drastic action was needed. Agreeing that some 30 per cent of the staff had to be sacrificed to save the jobs of the other 70 per cent, I wielded the surgical axe. *Outlook* Hindi had twenty-one staff members; we brought it down to eight. The monthly *Outlook Money* had twenty-odd staff, which was reduced to nine.

Letting go of people – imperilling their livelihoods – is never easy. But it had to be done, and I did so to the extent it was logical. For example, in *Outlook Traveller* – the monthly travel magazine from the Outlook stable – there were some half-a-dozen staff members designated for the sole purpose of bringing out travel guidebooks. Those guidebooks, mostly sponsored by the state governments, were irregular, and there were months when not a single guidebook came out. But the staff had to be paid salaries every month – with or without work. Meantime, staff meant for *Outlook Traveller* brought out the magazine once a month and were left with a lot of spare time. Obviously, we had staff in excess whom we had to let go.

But once I insisted on clarity about content, the demands to get rid of staff increased exponentially. Told to sack more people, this time from the *Outlook* main magazine, I put my foot down. No one told me anything at that point in time, but that I was no longer on the same page with the management was increasingly obvious. There were other issues over which we disagreed, including over the contours of *Outlook*'s planned digital-first strategy, and I found myself on a slippery slope.

At no point did any one of us raise voices or engage in a bitter argument. But the environment at work changed swiftly and silently. In sharp contrast to the smooth run that I had got used to, I suddenly found myself pushed against the wall. I struggled to be heard. Suddenly, my stock within the organization seemed to have plummeted and nothing I said cut any ice. My opinion ceased to matter, and I began to be cut out of the loop in matters of editorial calls, ranging from accepting resignations to making new appointments in critical positions.

Matters escalated within weeks. One thing led to another, and I went on leave, triggering speculation. Popular news websites such as www.newslaundry.com reported on my decision to go on leave, linking it with our 'Missing' cover. 'Is *Outlook* editor Ruben Banerjee being pushed out for a cover criticising the government', the headline of the Newslaundry report asked.[20] Others followed up, though I generally stayed quiet. 'I have gone on leave to clear my head and contemplate', I maintained and remained non-committal. The reports that appeared had some factual inaccuracies for want of a proper briefing, but I wasn't complaining since they portrayed me in a good light. I was portrayed as a kind of a martyr for the cause of honest and objective journalism.

Though I had simply gone on leave and not resigned, there seemingly was unanimity that I wouldn't be coming back. Even I began to seriously ponder my recent tumultuous past and wondered what the future might hold. Everyone who called me was almost certain that the roots of my misfortune lay in the 'Missing' cover and that the government had gone after me for the purpose of making an example of me. My well-wishers appeared to believe that there would be a cost every time someone takes on the powerful establishment.

I stayed mum through it all, not entirely certain what contributed to my current travails. For that matter, no BJP minister – but for the initial exchange I had with Dharmendra on the day I tweeted the cover – has been in touch with me since the issue came out. Several BJP national leaders who I was generally in touch with and were on somewhat friendly terms had also stayed away from me in its aftermath. One particular BJP functionary did send me messages, but more to make the point that I was wrong in running the cover. My attempts to defend it were all in vain, with the leader maintaining that I was a biased editor playing into the hands of those opposed to Prime Minister Modi.

Ironically, in the week that the situation unravelled rapidly for me, *Outlook* was getting ready to bring out an Independence Day special issue and I chased the supremo of RSS – the ideological fountainhead of the BJP – for a column on his idea of India on the country's seventy-fifth anniversary. Not knowing that I had possibly been bracketed as anti-BJP, I messaged Arun Kumar, the joint general secretary of the RSS, seeking his help to reach Mohan Bhagwat. Always open to various shades of opinion, I thought such a column would only add to the richness of *Outlook*'s special issue and pursued it to the best of my ability.

Kumar responded and put me in touch with someone else. A column by Bhagwat did not happen in the end but a lesser-known person who was heading an RSS-sponsored think tank wrote it. It did not make it to the magazine because the author lacked the heft, but we carried it online nonetheless to coincide with the Independence Day celebrations.

Being objective and fair-minded did not make much of a difference under the circumstances as I stood on the verge of losing my job and position. A colleague at *Outlook* who claimed to know a thing or two about organizational objectives offered a view. Many media houses in the country, he explained, were run by businessmen with interests in varied sectors – from petroleum products to real estate and energy. The owners of *Outlook* were known to be prominent builders who also had interests in hotels and insurance, among others. Other media barons, including Mukesh Ambani of Reliance and Ramoji Rao of *Eenadu*, owned many other things apart from newspapers and television stations. That, to the friend, was a bane that kept the media fettered. Unlike the BBC in the United Kingdom, which runs on public funding, the media in India is often subservient to the other business interests of their owners. The conglomerates they run are huge and the value of the media component in it could be comparatively small. Between protecting an empire worth Rs 50,000 crore and a media interest valued at Rs 50 crore, the former obviously gets priority. It could, as my friend elaborated, involve not antagonizing the government.

The argument over astronomical amounts of money being at stake at organizations made immense sense. Only, the price for being truthful at an individual level and pursuing objective journalism was proving to be as expensive.

3

THE STEEP CLIMB

'Get me tea', the middle-aged man in dhoti and panjabi (a Bengali kurta) said, pointing to a kettle. He was the chief reporter of a small Bengali newspaper, and I had gone to meet him at his office in Kolkata, referred to by a neighbour. I was still in college, but had already set my eyes on becoming a journalist. The problem was that I had no clear idea about the profession I wanted to be in and knew no one. For that matter, the only person my family or I knew who was remotely connected to the media was the hawker who gave us the newspaper every morning! I was desperate for a start, so there I was, in front of the chief reporter. Ordered to get tea, I picked up the kettle, went out and got him what he wanted. Having poured the tea in a glass, he took a sip, seemed satisfied and then asked me to come back after six months.

My first attempt at breaking into the profession bombed. Born in a middle-class Bengali family with neither a golden spoon in the mouth nor the Queen's doctor helping my mother bring me into the world – as a famous editor of our time was – I started out small, insignificant and struggling all the way. My fascination with journalism began in the late 1970s while still in high school, when I accidentally met a reporter of the now-defunct *Surya* magazine that was run by Maneka Gandhi, wife of the Gandhi dynasty scion, Sanjay. Her proximity to power made her much sought after then.

That Maneka Gandhi was the editor was the magazine's claim to fame. It found greater popularity when in one of its issues, it splashed what it claimed were 'compromising' pictures of the son of Babu Jagjivan Ram, the veteran Congress leader who had fallen out with Indira Gandhi. Since *Surya* enjoyed enormous visibility, the magazine's reporter in Kolkata, Partha Sarathi Kar, who was also Maneka's batchmate in Jawaharlal Nehru University (JNU), carried a lot of clout, at least among the Congressmen of the state. Bunking my classes, I would hang around at the reporter's house for hours every day, and what I regularly saw dazzled me. Leaders of the party – then Congress (I) – visited him regularly. Even some chief ministers, such as Nar Bahadur Bhandari of Sikkim, came calling at times. The high-profile visits left an impression on me, and I wholeheartedly wished to be a journalist.

I was watching a journalist in flesh and blood for the first time in my life, and that he was so influential impressed me in no small measure. One day, he wished to join the Congress (I) and become an important functionary. Somen Mitra, the then West Bengal Youth Congress (I) chief, readily acquiesced. That same night, the news bulletin on Doordarshan announced that Partha Sarathi Kar had been appointed a vice-president of the state unit.

I was more impressed, and I desperately wished to be like Kar. He took me under his wings and sent me on errands – essentially to go out and get quotes from people or gather information on incidents he was reporting on. Though in his early forties, Kar – Parthada to me – was not in good health. His kidneys failed, and he was put on dialysis, and he passed away not long after. My journey as a budding journalist seemed to have been halted even before it had taken off.

So, I started out afresh, my hopes for a break coalescing around anyone or everyone – big or small – that my limited circle of friends and acquaintances claimed to know in the media. That explained why I presented myself before the chief reporter of the Bengali paper one fine day. He sent me back rather curtly, but I had got used to rejection by then.

Even so, I persisted in pursuing my dream and kept getting rejected. I wrote articles – mostly on inconsequential subjects such as the list of best tailors in Kolkata and the restaurant serving the most delicious biryani – and sent them to various publications around the country – but nothing appeared anywhere. Only the rejection slips stating that my article has been found unfit for use kept piling up. It continued that way for almost a year, and my parents began to get anxious. They had reason to. Though not exactly rich, my father earned well as a businessman. He ran a wholesale coal depot and a pharmaceutical shop. But somewhere, something went wrong, and his business went bust. He stopped earning, never to recover.

We fell on bad times. Thereafter, we lived on borrowed money, with two of my father's best friends pledging to support the education of my brother and me. But the going got tough, with many of our relatives even refusing to invite us to family functions since we apparently didn't have proper clothes suited for occasions such as weddings.

Time certainly was running out as I floundered to find my feet. It helped the family that the career of my brother – an extremely meritorious student – had taken off. He began to pay back the money we had borrowed over the years, but that didn't lessen the pressure on me to come good quickly. I got lucky then. I wrote up a report on how some blood donors of the city had turned professional and were donating blood every second day at various hospitals for some money and snacks. I profiled some of them, and a friend – an amateur photographer – took the pictures. Reasonably satisfied with the piece, I offered it to the *Amrita Bazar Patrika*, the Kolkata daily, which had an illustrious past but was well past its prime. I met an editor who seemed interested. Instead of rejecting it outright, he kept it – and then followed a long period of silence.

I waited as if my life depended on the article's publication. Weeks turned into months, yet nothing happened. I kept visiting the *Patrika* office, but the editor wouldn't make any promises. I once again turned to someone a friend claimed was a well-connected journalist. I began visiting him persistently, seeking his help to find out the fate of my article. Looking back, my desperation then seems ridiculous. But I pursued it with single-minded devotion.

Finally, one day, the journalist my friend had referred me to pulled a fast one. He said the *Patrika* had decided against publishing my piece. It finally didn't make the cut, he claimed. I was devastated. But the very next day – it was a Sunday – a friend from the neighbourhood came running, waving that day's *Patrika*.

My story, titled 'Bloody Business', had appeared on the cover of the daily's weekly magazine.

I was on cloud nine and perhaps higher. I began writing reports more furiously and regularly. By then, the earlier rejections had given me a fair idea about which periodical accepted what kind of stories, and soon I forged a workable relationship with *Current*, a weekly tabloid coming out of Mumbai, then Bombay. *Current* gave me no money, but I wrote for them week after week. In no time, they began treating me as their Calcutta correspondent. It didn't matter that I was unpaid. I was simply happy to contribute and see my byline in print.

My confidence grew. Some months later, I noticed a small advertisement in a Kolkata newspaper that a Hyderabad-based media group planned to launch an English daily and was looking to hire trainee journalists. I applied for the position. But – as it turned out to be a disconcerting pattern later in my career – I didn't crack it the first time. The *Eenadu* group headed by Ramoji Rao – famous now for the state-of-the-art Ramoji Film City in Hyderabad – called me for a test and interview and set a date.

Unfortunately, it coincided with my graduation examination, and my hopes for a formal job were dashed. I rued my fate till they advertised again some months later, and I re-applied. This time I was luckier. I took the test and was short-listed for an interview with Ramoji Rao the next day. I passed that too and was offered the position of a trainee reporter with the soon-to-be-launched *Newstime* newspaper in Hyderabad. I was finally on course to becoming a professional journalist.

Newstime bombed and folded up a couple of years later, but the one year or so that I spent there offered great learnings. The paper was mostly made up of rookie reporters, and it meant we were allowed to report on all things important, including politics. I got off to a flying start – more by chance. All singles, some of my young colleagues and I went for a drink at a bar in Hyderabad's Panjagutta neighbourhood one evening, without knowing what lay in store for us.

It turned out to be a strip joint, where women on the stage danced nude under pulsating strobe lights to the accompaniment of loud music. As we ogled, the police raided the place and took away most of the girls – some extremely beautiful. The show stopped abruptly, and we came back disappointed. But the next day, my spirits soared unexpectedly. Crime happened to be one of the beats I covered, and that involved visiting the city courts every day. The day following the raid, I was at the courts next to the famous Charminar monument in the old city and was startled to find the police producing the women detained during the previous night's raid. But then the girls brought to the court were different – they were not half as beautiful as the ones taken away! Obviously, the girls had been changed, possibly for money, and the judge was being taken for a ride. I rushed back to the office to write what I had seen. The first-hand account made for a good read, and my first boss saw me as a great investigative reporter in the making.

I kept getting drawn into situations unwittingly, mostly to my advantage. Not many weeks had passed since I joined *Newstime*, when I was covering a lawyers' protest outside the state assembly that turned ugly. The police swung their batons and rather inexplicably targeted C. Kesavalu, *Eenadu*'s photographer. A man of few words, Kesavalu normally let his pictures speak and had made a reputation for himself. Many credited him with helping N.T. Rama Rao, the matinee idol, capture the popular imagination in his first campaign to become chief minister of then undivided Andhra Pradesh.

Eenadu and Ramoji Rao backed NTR wholeheartedly, and it was Kesavulu who accompanied the freshly-minted politician as he campaigned in his refurbished vehicle christened the Chaitanya Ratham. NTR stopped to take a roadside bath or eat at a small restaurant, and Kesavalu was there to take photographs, which *Eenadu* splashed on its front page. But that day, when the lawyers of the state with NTR as the chief minister demonstrated, I spotted the police beating him and rushed to his aid. We both were physically lifted and thrown in the back of a police jeep.

Hit on the head, Kesavalu was unconscious. The word spread, and opposition legislators inside the state assembly staged a noisy walkout, even as we were driven from one police station to another. Even NTR was supposedly agitated over the police action. Passions rose, and lawyers of Hyderabad and Secunderabad went on a strike. Some political parties called for a state-wide protest the next day, and a harried government, forced on the backfoot, ordered a judicial enquiry. The next day, I found myself on the front pages, alongside Kesavalu.

I spent my time with *Newstime*, seeking to make a greater mark. The opportunities were many, with Hyderabad – then the capital of undivided Andhra Pradesh – at the centre of immense political turmoil. Indira Gandhi, as the powerful Prime Minister, was attempting to oust the popular NTR and had initiated a political coup. True to his movie background, NTR resorted to unmatched drama. He cut short a foreign visit and returned to the city in a wheelchair, projecting himself as a victim who has been gravely wronged. Popular support was with him, and Telugus took to the streets in unprecedented numbers. Indira Gandhi's plot was foiled, and NTR staged a resounding comeback after having been unseated temporarily. I was among the lucky few recording the fast-paced developments for posterity.

But *Newstime* wasn't a very happy place, and I sought greener pastures. An obvious choice was the *Indian Express* – the multi-edition newspaper that had an edition in Hyderabad. I turned up with no appointment at the office of the paper's resident editor. But as was the case with me all through my later career, I was shooed away the first time. How dare you come in unannounced? The elderly editor literally chased me away. Some months passed, and I tried my luck again, sending the same editor my CV. By then, he had forgotten about our first meeting and responded enthusiastically. He agreed to meet me and asked for some of my writings. He was impressed with what he saw, and an offer to join the *Express* as a reporter in the Hyderabad bureau soon followed. I took my first step towards something better and bigger.

Working at the *Express* was fun, but not without hiccups. Recruited directly by the resident editor, the chief reporter nursed a grudge, at least initially. It seemed I could do nothing right as he invariably tore into whatever I wrote. Then, one day, I saw him melt before my eyes. Asked to report on something innocuous, I submitted my piece and waited, trembling for the chief reporter to go through it. He ran his eyes through it, liked what he read and smiled. Since that day, I became the favourite of the chief reporter, feared for his foul temper. On days he was angry, he would give all the reporters a dressing down one by one. When my turn came, he somehow would soften up remarkably. 'Bangali babu, can you get us some good exclusive stories,' he would meekly implore. Under his benevolent gaze, I thrived.

Two years flew by, and I flourished as a city reporter. During the mid-1980s, there were not as many non-Telugu reporters in

Hyderabad as there are today. Being a kind of rarity, I found ready acceptance. Even NTR as the chief minister, who had the habit of holding press conferences at 4 a.m. at the ashram he lived in on the city's outskirts, would switch to Hindi when he spotted me. Never short of drama, NTR kept us engaged. At one point, he began sporting a turban, and we as reporters vainly attempted to figure out why. Rumours had it that a tantric had recommended the chief minister keep a lemon on his head to propitiate the gods, which NTR kept hidden from the public eye by wearing the turban. Married and with grown-up children, NTR never tired of piquing public curiosity. He began to live with a lady named Lakshmi Parvathi and married her some years later, adding further colour to an eventful life.

My initial years as a reporter, though not spectacular, wasn't uneventful either. Luck seemed to be on my side, without which I would have abruptly lost my job when I decided to bunk office one night and go to a movie with some of my colleagues. At the time, communal riots would periodically break out in old Hyderabad, plunging the city into chaos and uncertainty. The two most prominent community leaders were A. Narendra of the BJP and Sultan Salahuddin Owaisi, the late father of Asaduddin Owaisi, who is now head of the All India Majlis-e-Ittehadul Muslimeen (AIMIM). Narendra and the elder Owaisi were reported to be great friends, meeting and dining regularly. But, on the ground, riots kept recurring, with rival communities going at each other at frequent intervals.

I was working in the office one night during such a charged period when some *Express* colleagues – from the editorial desk – popped into our reporting bureau and invited me to join them for a late-night movie. It was past 8 p.m., and I was standing in for the crime reporter who was on leave. It meant I had to call up more than fifty police stations of the twin cities and check for any untoward incidents until the newspaper went to press around 2 a.m. I had been doing it for the past several days, and that night was no different. Since things seemed to be quiet, I took the bait. I decided to close shop early and left with my colleagues for the movie. I was in for a shock the next morning.

I woke up to find that every other paper in town – with the exception of the *Express* – had leads on their front pages reporting the violence that had erupted the previous night, post 9 p.m. An MLA had been killed, triggering large-scale violence in the old city, forcing the authorities to clamp a curfew. It was mayhem. I held my head in grief, having missed such an important story. Those were pre-mobile days, and I did not have a landline at home. It allowed me to go incommunicado. I didn't go to the office for the next few days. By the time I went back to work, my chief reporter had calmed down considerably. All was forgotten, and I continued to be his favourite.

Some more months passed, and he came up with a great offer. *Express* then was an undivided newspaper chain – unlike now with the *Indian Express* in north India and the *New Indian Express* in southern regions – and correspondents based across the states contributed to all editions, giving them unmatched readership and reach. Undoubtedly fond of and extremely concerned about my well-being, the chief reporter suggested that I go to Bhubaneswar – the capital of Odisha (then spelt Orissa) – as the state correspondent since the person who held the position had left.

'Bangali Babu, you should go. You will be closer home to Calcutta', he insisted. The move was undoubtedly a giant leap – from being just one of the many reporters in a city bureau, here I was becoming the sole representative of a newspaper chain in an entire state – something that came to define and impact my later career unmistakably. But when I initially agreed to the transfer, the only thought that I harboured was that home, Calcutta, was only an overnight journey from Bhubaneswar.

In my mid-twenties, I landed up in Odisha in early 1987, particularly excited to find that the numerous sweetmeat shops of Bhubaneswar offered a wide range of Bengali sweets, rasagollas included – something of a rarity in Hyderabad. I took to Odisha with the ease of a duck to water. Odia seemed almost similar to my own mother tongue, and I quickly learnt to read and write in it. I began relishing Odia literature, beginning with *Chha Mana Atha Guntha* (Six Acres and a Third), a seminal work by Odisha's most revered litterateur, Fakir Mohan Senapati.

While still new to the state, a phone call one day from someone with a gruff voice jolted me out of my comfort zone. I was in my *Express* office-cum-residence when the gentleman called. I gathered that he was extremely unhappy with a report we had carried in the paper that morning and was voicing his displeasure. 'You come to my office now', he howled and put down the phone. Not knowing who had called, I sat tight till the phone rang again after about half an hour. 'What happened? You haven't come. I am waiting for you,' the caller now virtually yelled. Still unsure who he was, I rather sheepishly asked about his identity. 'I am Biju Patnaik', he shouted in disgust.

There was no one in Odisha, or possibly in the entire country, who did not know who Biju Patnaik was. An ex-industrialist and a freedom fighter known for his daredevilry, he was part of folklore. Extremely close to India's first Prime Minister, Jawaharlal Nehru, the tall and towering Patnaik had become larger than life with his exploits, including that as a Royal Indian Air Force pilot who flew in the face of grave danger in 1947 to rescue Indonesian premier Sutan Sjahrir, who had been put under house arrest by the Dutch colonial government.

He gradually gave up his businesses and became a full-time politician – first becoming the state's chief minister for a couple of years in the early 1960s and then a Union minister during the Janata government rule between 1977 and 1980. By far the most well-known politician in the state – irrespective of whether he was in power or out of it – Patnaik was leader of the Opposition at the time, and everyone was in awe of him.

What followed his second call was comical. Heeding his command, I rode my two-wheeler to his office in the leafy Forest Park neighbourhood and presented myself before him. 'You kept me waiting. You know who I am? I am Biju Patnaik, 6 feet 2 inches tall', he said in his trademark expansive style. Still not overwhelmed, I retorted, 'I am Ruben Banerjee, 5 feet 5 inches tall.' A hushed silence followed, broken a few moments later by his loud laughter. Biju Babu – as he was commonly known – found my response extremely unusual and funny.

Our bonding – between that of a politician and a reporter – grew, helped by the fact that the Congress government in power in the state was extremely unpopular and most of my reports were anti-government. With Arun Shourie as its famous chief editor, the *Express* revelled in exposing the establishment, and I played my role from my territory in Odisha. There was a lot to write about – mostly on mounting despair, backbreaking poverty and unending claims of starvation deaths. Kalahandi, an interior district in south-western Odisha, was being described globally as India's Ethiopia, and there was no dearth of human interest stories. We travelled extensively and reported frenetically, which invariably the opposition legislators, led by Biju Patnaik, weaponized to turn the tables on the beleaguered state government both inside and outside the state assembly. The going could not have been any better for a young reporter trying to find his feet, until I found myself suddenly transferred to Kolkata.

I was stunned, shocked and unhappy. So was Biju Babu, who called up Shourie to express his displeasure. Looking back, such a show of support from a politician wasn't desirable. But I felt extreme gratitude then. Nothing worked to stall my transfer, and my friends gave me a tearful farewell sweetened with a gift in the shape of a portable typewriter. I settled down in Kolkata unhappily and missed Odisha every waking moment. It was rather strange and ironic. While in Hyderabad, I had been terribly homesick and dreamt of coming back to my home city as a reporter. I had tried my best repeatedly but in vain. Among others, I had met the editor of the *Statesman*, but it turned out to be futile. I applied for a reporter's job with *Amrita Bazar Patrika* when the now-defunct newspaper advertised. I paid for my ticket and travelled all the way to appear for an interview at an appointed date and hour, only to find that no one in the office knew about it. I spent the whole day outside, waiting to be called in. No one called.

The Kolkata days at the *Express* were insufferable, as I longed to be back in Odisha. More irony followed. About nine months later, Shourie called me to Delhi for a chat. I arrived, and he ushered me into his large, dimly-lit room with extreme warmth. 'You are an extremely fine reporter', he said as I tentatively took my seat. The camaraderie lasted no more than two minutes. Shourie said I was being transferred back to Odisha as the person who had succeeded me hadn't proven very successful.

This was something I wished to hear, but my original hurt over being transferred out so ignominiously in the first place rankled. 'But Sir, am I a football which can be kicked around like this', I blurted. From all sugar and honey, Shourie now shook in rage. 'You are the worst I have seen', he shouted, summarily dismissing me. As I walked out, I saw some senior colleagues in the corridor and lingered to talk to them. But not for long. Shourie came from behind and literally chased me out. I was soon standing on the other side of the road outside the *Express* office, which was then on Delhi's Fleet Street – Bahadur Shah Zafar Marg. I found myself with no place to go.

I still had a day left in Delhi, and an old friend who lived in the city tried to comfort me. He suggested that I try my luck the next day at *India Today* – then the country's premier news magazine. He brought me to the magazine's Connaught Place office and waited downstairs as I made my way up the narrow stairs to seek a meeting with one of the magazine's top editors. I did not know anyone in person, but I had heard a lot about Prabhu Chawla, and once at the reception, I asked whether I could meet him. I was asked to wait. Then after about half an hour, I got my call.

'*Aa gaya? Naukri chahiye?* (You've made it? Do you want a job?)', Prabhu spoke the moment I stepped in, startling me. It seemed he was already aware of me, or at least my bylines, and things moved fast. I was quickly taken to meet the other editors, including the owner-editor Aroon Purie. The interviews over, I was asked to wait for their response.

I returned to Kolkata and waited. Weeks and months passed, and I heard nothing from *India Today*. My *Indian Express* transfer order to Bhubaneswar meanwhile gathered dust, and I couldn't delay it beyond a point. I got back to Odisha – half pleased and half hurt – to a warm welcome from my Odia friends, who now insisted in a lighter vein that I return the portable typewriter they had given me as a parting gift. I resumed where I had left off, and life was good again. The extremely unpopular government of J.B. Patnaik had made way for a new Congress dispensation in the state, and Lok Sabha elections in 1989 ultimately won by V.P. Singh's Janata Dal and allies added to the excitement. There was a change of guard in Odisha as well, with Biju Patnaik sweeping back to power after a long gap of more than two decades in state elections in 1990.

My life changed too. A couple of months after I had returned to Bhubaneswar, the office phone rang, and to my surprise, it was Prabhu. 'You left Kolkata without even informing us,' he said. 'I have been searching for your contact details since then,' he complained in jest. He had an offer for me in front of him, and I readily agreed. I joined *India Today* within days, continuing on in Bhubaneswar. I was happy despite struggling to make the transition from a newspaper to a magazine reporter. The task at hand seemed daunting, and I was overwhelmed in every which way, including my first plane ride. Called to the Delhi office for an editorial meeting, I was rattled by what I saw and heard. Seeing famous journalists and photographers such as Inderjit Badhwar, Dilip Bobb, Shekhar Gupta, Tarun Tejpal and Raghu Rai at work from close quarters, my small-town instincts gave me an inferiority complex. I felt I was not cut out for the high-flying world of *India Today*.

For the first year or so, I barely managed to get into the widely read magazine – a single column here and a one page there. I did nothing of consequence, but the editors persisted with me. After about a year, in 1991, they asked me to relocate to Kolkata, where I was subsequently joined by another reporter who became a life-long friend, Soutik Biswas. The two of us were tasked with covering a bigger region – West Bengal, Odisha, the northeastern states and the neighbouring countries of Bangladesh and Nepal. I gradually found my feet and increasingly found space in the magazine. But it was baptism by fire. Asked to go to Bangladesh to cover the general elections under way there, I was caught unprepared. I didn't have a passport. By the time I pulled strings and hurriedly got one – an Indo-Bangladesh passport valid just for seven days – most international journalists were on their way back from Dhaka. Fortunately, *India Today* was a fortnightly then, and I had time to make up for the late start.

I would visit Odisha often, covering developments in the state and chasing unending human-interest stories waiting to be written about. Poverty and hunger stayed the dominant theme of stories that came out of Odisha then. As also, reports of children being sold by their parents on account of penury reportedly for the 'price of a plate of chicken'.[1] Biju Babu was the chief minister, but I fell afoul of his most powerful bureaucrat, Pyari Mohan Mohapatra. True to his cavalier style, Biju Babu had exhorted the people to beat up officials who they thought were corrupt and inefficient, but only after sending him an intimation. Just a postcard or a telegram would do; no approval was needed, the chief minister said.

Some telegrams poured in concerning Mohapatra, and I reported that. Headstrong and an egoist, Mohapatra took strong exception. He sued *India Today* and me, both for criminal and civil defamation. He sought rupees one crore in damages. It threatened to irrevocably damage my reputation, but, fortunately, the matter was settled out of court a few years later. It taught me a valuable lesson: one needs to be cautious irrespective of one's connections in high places.

Back in my headquarters in Kolkata, I gradually found acceptance. Remember the dhoti-panjabi clad gentleman whom I had approached for a job, and who had dismissively asked me to get tea? I ran into him at Writers' Buildings, the then seat of West Bengal government. I didn't have to say a word – I was with *India Today*, while he continued to be the representative of a small Bengali paper – and the gentleman was visibly embarrassed. He tried making amends by being extra nice, and we later became friends. There was also this funny incident when I got a call from one Mrs Banerjee of the *Statesman*. The paper – steeped in history and rich in legacy – organized an annual event. It was an important occasion in the city's calendar, and Mrs Banerjee wished to come over and invite me for its coverage in *India Today*. I said yes, and a day later, she walked in. The moment she saw me, she was reminded of when she'd seen me before.

A couple of years ago, I had been to the *Statesman* to meet the editor, seeking a job, who then asked me to go to the anteroom and write a 1,000-word essay on Bofors, the controversial arms deal that was the biggest story of the time. The editor's secretary was none other than Mrs Banerjee, who had taken me to the other room, given me a pen and paper and had promised to come back after an hour to collect the essay from me. Left alone and unable to write a coherent line, I walked out through the back door. But meeting now after a couple of years, Mrs Banerjee recollected the earlier encounter and said: 'Oh, you are the same person. Where is the essay? I am still waiting.' 'I am still writing it', I replied. Both of us burst out laughing, bereft of any rancour.

Life followed a comfortable pattern, punctuated with long spells of free time. *India Today* was still a fortnightly, and it meant there was plenty of idle time between two issues. That changed after a new kid on the block – *Outlook* – hit the stands and created more than a flutter in 1995. Some *India Today* colleagues had crossed over to join the new magazine – planned as a weekly – and one day, one of them called, introducing me to one of the top editors of the proposed magazine. The editor held out a job offer – would I be willing to join as their reporter in Kolkata, he asked. I outright said no. *India Today* was still at the peak of its popularity and promised a stable job and salary – so important for me at that point in time. Also, I wasn't impressed with the name of the new magazine. *Outlook* – what kind of name is that? – I wondered to myself, immensely happy at turning down the offer off-hand.

But *Outlook* got off to a flying start, its launch issue being a mega hit. Suddenly, *India Today* had competition. Sitting in distant Kolkata, we felt the heat too. A couple of months later, *India Today* changed into a weekly, presumably reluctant to let *Outlook* occupy the space unchallenged. It was also the time when television news was coming of age, and a fortnightly magazine was seen to be losing in topicality. Once we became a weekly, we came under pressure. The free time we enjoyed between issues separated by two weeks became a thing of the past. We got busy chasing tighter deadlines. It turned infinitely worse for me a year later, towards the end of 1996. I ran into problems with Prabhu, the editor who had given me the big break at *India Today*. A few years after I had joined, Prabhu left *India Today* to join *Indian Express* as the editor. He took away with him the people of his choice. He met me in Kolkata and offered me a job too. An offer letter was hurriedly typed out and handed over to me. But later, I had a rethink and let go of the offer, preferring to continue with *India Today*. Towards the end of 1996, Prabhu returned to *India Today* as editor, and my troubles began.

For some inexplicable reasons, I found myself suddenly persona non grata. Nothing I did seemed to make the cut, and for six months or so, I failed to find any space in the magazine. I was also superseded during the period by someone who, ironically, had been approaching me for a while for a job with *India Today*. But once appointed as my senior in the Kolkata bureau, he made my life more difficult, and I had no place to hide. I made renewed efforts to find a job, but failed. The *Statesman*, under a new editor, said they couldn't afford me as the paper was incurring losses. *Telegraph* too refused, with its editor saying he was unsure about the quality of my writing. I kept my head down, waiting for a change in my fortunes. It came in the shape of a transfer back to Bhubaneswar towards the end of 1997.

Apparently, my plight evoked compassion among some *India Today* editors and they felt I needed a hand. They petitioned Prabhu and managed to impress upon him that I was always good when it came to covering Odisha and that I was being wasted in Kolkata. Prabhu somehow agreed, and I was back in Odisha – for the third time and what turned out to be the most productive years of my reporting career. It laid the foundation for what I would go on to achieve later.

More seasoned and mature, I excelled in my latest Odisha stint – not because I was excellent, but primarily because the competition I faced was poor. Press handouts and what politicians said generally formed the backbone of the journalism practised by the local media, and as and when I strayed from the normal practice, it made me look exceptionally good.

One story that covered me in glory was how spouses of influential bureaucrats were circumventing rules and regulations to avoid being transferred out of their comfort zones in Bhubaneswar and Cuttack as teachers at government colleges. Rules stipulated that teachers should be transferred every few years and thousands of teachers, far less connected and serving in interiors of the state, waited for their turns to be in the two cities. But the bureaucrat-spouses denied them the opportunity. They stayed on in their positions for years and decades, at times getting themselves transferred from the morning section of the college to the day section to side-step rules. The story in *India Today* – with names and examples – triggered an outcry. That a journalist had the courage to name so many influential people in one story was a cause of widespread wonderment.

Though poor and considered backward, Odisha suddenly was awash with stories. Biju Babu had died, and his socialite son, Naveen, had taken up his mantle. He soon floated his own political party – the Biju Janata Dal – and Odisha was caught up in a political swirl that threatened the Congress dispensation in the state. One thing followed the other, and Odisha hit the national headlines incessantly, allowing me a golden run. A lady by the name Anjana Mishra[2] was fighting a divorce battle when the state advocate general – a confidant of the then chief minister J.B. Patnaik – called her for a meeting. She came out alleging a sexual assault, triggering a scandal that raged for years. It turned murkier when the director general of police told the court under oath that there existed a nexus between the chief minister and the advocate general, both of whom shared an interest in women. And when the lady was waylaid one night and gangraped, the state was hit by an even bigger scandal.[3]

There was a surprisingly steady stream of outrages, and one such occurred in the January of 1999 when an Australian missionary, Graham Staines, was murdered along with his two young children by a mob led by a self-proclaimed Hindu zealot, Dara Singh.[4] Staines – who ran a leprosy home in Baripada of Mayurbhanj district – and his two children were sleeping out in the open in their jeep when the mob set them ablaze. It lit a global outcry, with even the Vatican stepping in with condemnation. Staines, the mob suspected, was secretly involved in proselytization – a charge that was never proven. But the bloodcurdling crime underlined the communal divide that was already running deep in a state where the BJP was struggling to make a mark. And I got my chance to do my first cover story for *India Today*.

More cover stories followed in close succession. As the country's most wanted fugitive, Dara Singh, caught popular imagination and tracking his growing nuisance value made for fascinating reading. Even as the police launched a massive hunt, armed with night vision goggles and heat-imaging gadgets, he went on to kill more. It meant more stories – each more interesting than the previous one. Dara, it turned out, was originally from Uttar Pradesh and was known as Rabindra Pal Singh. He strategically took the name of Dara Singh[5] – after the famous wrestler of yesteryears – to portray a macho image and strike instant fear when he came to Odisha for what turned out to be his misguided religious putsch. The hunt for him was no less interesting. Once, a police patrol found a man drunk and sprawled senseless in the middle of the road. The cops carried him to the side and left, only to realize later that he was none other than Dara. But by the time they returned, Dara had come back to his senses and walked away.

There was no dearth of Dara stories that kept me busy right until he was finally nabbed. Once in jail, I sought to interview him. But the Odisha government wouldn't allow me to do that, and I knocked the courts for permission. The high court in Cuttack ruled in my favour, and a precedent was thereby set for journalists to interview undertrials. Soon afterwards, I triumphantly went to the Baripada jail to meet Dara, and what he told me was startling.

Contrary to popular perception, Dara said he wasn't part of the RSS-sponsored Bajrang Dal. He was more of a freelance religious fanatic who was impressed the most by Bal Thackeray of the Shiv Sena. He also expressed no remorse for killing the Staines.[6]

I, too, had no regrets about being in Odisha, though the state had the singular misfortune of being visited by one disaster after the other – man-made and natural. Before 1999 gave way to 2000, a huge cyclone – described then as the Super Cyclone, since the practice of giving names to storms was yet not in vogue – roared up the shores of the Bay of Bengal and struck the unsuspecting and unprepared state. The storm brought incessant rains and extremely strong winds – so powerful that even coconuts snapped and flew off trees – and Odisha found itself bent and broken.

In Ersama of Jagatsinghpur district in coastal Odisha, the storm scooped up the sea and three successive waves came rushing inland for as far as some 20 km.[7] It swept away everything in its path – houses, trees and human beings. By the time the storm abated and the sea waters receded, some 10,000 people lay dead. Those who survived were left hungry and destitute. First to crumble in the battering that the state received was the administration of the then chief minister, Giridhar Gamang. The normally garrulous chief minister was left speechless by the enormity of the disaster. All modes of communication were knocked out by the storm, and Gamang himself was stranded in his official residence, with its gates blocked by fallen trees and without electricity. The police reported large-scale desertions from its ranks and anarchy swept the state. Odisha found itself adrift on a sea of helplessness.[8]

As tens of thousands of homeless and hapless Odias fought – first over relief and then over rehabilitation – one of the biggest beneficiaries of the enormous calamity was me. The super cyclone was a global story and *India Today* ran three successive covers on the tragedy in its immediate aftermath. A devastated Odisha opened up immense opportunities for journalists, and we found stories in whichever direction we looked – from stories of courage, exemplified by Aarti Kandi, a young girl who clung to a tree to survive as the sea rushed in and then retreated, washing away her family, to acts of cowardice when marauding mobs exploited the chaos to loot passing trucks carrying anything from cement to condoms.

Living in Bhubaneswar, I experienced the havoc first-hand, despite being miles away from the eye of the storm. Our high-rise building swayed violently, and the city wore a bombed-out look for days, with electric poles twisted and trees felled. What I saw, felt and later found out, provided meat for the first book I authored a year later – *The Orissa Tragedy: A Cyclone's Year of Calamity*.[9] It found critical acclaim, including a positive review in *Time* magazine. But what I reported in the immediate aftermath – the second cover story for *India Today* – is more remembered today.

An affable tribal leader from Koraput in southern Odisha, Giridhar Gamang was already at sea when the super cyclone hit his unsuspecting state. He had been elected a member of parliament repeatedly – no less than eight times – and was also the junior telecom minister during Rajiv Gandhi's premiership. The telecom revolution that the country witnessed in the 1980s gave Gamang a halo, though people who knew better credited it to the technocrat Sam Pitroda, also from Odisha.

Gamang's stock rose, and when the Congress high command finally decided to give the boot to J.B. Patnaik in the wake of the Staines' murder and the Anjana Mishra rape case, Gamang became the chief minister. Though an experienced MP who mostly transited through Bhubaneswar to go to Delhi or return to Koraput, he hadn't lived in Bhubaneswar and knew little of the capital city's machinations. Worse still, he was a poor administrator despite being well-intentioned. He allowed himself to be surrounded by a coterie, and suddenly, people not very well known in the city's elite circles came to call the shots.

The coterie included Gamang's son, Shishir. Shishir's clout skyrocketed as his father became the chief minister. But like the father, the son, too, didn't have his own circle in the city. He looked for friends after settling down at his father's official residence and somehow gravitated towards me. He visited me regularly and almost every second night we would be at some hotel or other dining together. Knowing the son guaranteed unhindered access to the chief minister's home and all that happened therein. It included fascinating details of what Gamang did the night before the storm gathered ferocious speed over the Bay of Bengal and came crashing the next day.

Everyone knew the advancing cyclone was exceptionally strong, but none could guess the extent of damage it could wreak. Gamang was tense and had closeted himself with three tantriks – shamans who dabbled in black magic – the night before. Called by none other than the chief minister himself, the tantriks competed with each other to please him. One said Gamang's star constellations were such that the storm would hit his chest and return to the sea; another said the gale would blow high over Odisha and spare the state much damage on the ground, while the third predicted that it would split into two, with one heading towards West Bengal and the other hurtling towards Andhra Pradesh. Gamang went to sleep somewhat convinced his state would be safe.

The tantriks were proven woefully wrong, and *India Today*'s second cover story two weeks after the storm struck, catalogued in great detail the failings of the government. More damaging was the cover. It had a picture of Gamang with a headline: 'Gamang Should Go'! Working out of powerless Bhubaneswar, I wrote my reports longhand on candle-lit nights and sent them to *India Today* office through a passenger who travelled to Delhi by air after flight services gradually resumed. Raj Chengappa – the magazine's current editor – anchored the story.[10]

One late night, he called to say Gamang wouldn't survive the cover. He will go, Raj said. As expected, Gamang went some days later, replaced by another chief minister for a few months before the storm-battered state voted for a new assembly. I had reasons to cheer but checked my emotions. Convalescing from a bad bout of illness, Shishir Gamang called from his hospital bed to complain about what he felt was personal betrayal. He said something like 'Et tu, Brute?'

The Congress was doomed in Odisha, and in came Naveen Patnaik as the new chief minister a few months later, riding on a huge wave of popular goodwill. A socialite in his earlier life, who spent most of his time in the rarefied circles of Delhi and abroad, Patnaik spoke no Odia. Though people rooted for him because he was Biju Babu's son, he was very much a stranger to the state he came to rule. I was a stranger to him. However, as luck would have it, my immediate boss in *India Today*, Swapan Dasgupta, knew him well and took me to meet the new chief minister. A man of perfect etiquette, Patnaik reciprocated warmly.

At a time when very few had access to him, the doors of Naveen Niwas – the sprawling home Biju Babu had built and named after his younger son – were always open to me. I would drive down every now and then, hoping to be stopped. But every time I went, the guards and waiters at the chief minister's house would stand up and let me in. Inside, Naveen Patnaik tolerated me, though I had a distinct impression that he didn't really like me. By then, he had told me that his ties with *India Today* went back decades – since the time when Aroon Purie's sister, Madhu Trehan, had first conceptualized the magazine and Patnaik had contributed his thoughts. Whether he liked me or not, he put up with *India Today*'s man in Odisha.

It helped me immensely. The fact that I breezed in and out of the chief minister's home with ease was duly noticed, and the word spread. I came to be seen as someone close to the CM, and my new-found reputation preceded me wherever I went, including when I called on an important minister hoping to get some information that was a closely guarded secret. The minister jumped up on seeing me, deciding to share not just the information but all the relevant files as well.

Journalism had never been this easy, with ministers and bureaucrats virtually at my beck and call. The access I enjoyed gave rise to unintended results. Some ruling-party men looking for plum positions made a beeline for me, while government officials pestered me with incessant requests for choice transfers. While I chose to let my journalism do the talking, my fabled access became the talk of the town. To many, I was an unabashed Patnaik-acolyte

– despite the anti-government stories[11] that I continued to write at regular intervals.[12]

Though a member of the local media, I wasn't really considered one by others who made up the crowd then. My run-ins with them had started early, soon after I had landed up in the state as the *Indian Express* correspondent. J.B. Patnaik was the chief minister then, and he ran a very tight ship, cracking down on critics and rewarding those who praised him. The media was largely beholden to him for small favours, from subsidised government accommodation to advertisements. One journalist had stepped out of line, and the Patnaik administration punished him by throwing him out of government accommodation, citing a three-day break in his accreditation as he changed jobs.

The action against the journalist smacked of vendetta, and I did several front-page reports for *Indian Express*, giving out examples and names of other journalists who had been allowed to retain their government quarters for years without accreditation. One of them was allowed to retain for years the sprawling house allotted in one of Bhubaneswar's best addresses to his late journalist-father until he found a job and became a journalist himself. The Editors Guild of India took note and sent a three-member team comprising Kuldip Nayar, K.R. Malkani and S. Sahay for an on-the-spot fact-finding mission. My reports were widely quoted by the editors in their report titled 'J.B. Patnaik's Orissa – the Story of Carrot and Stick'. The expose earned me a lot of displeasure locally.

It escalated into veritable enmity when a report of mine in *India Today* punched gaping holes in the stories the other journalists from the state regularly did on alleged starvation deaths. Odisha had always been poor and the country's top editors felt that nothing important ever happened there except poverty, deprivation and the occasional disaster. That being the overwhelming mindset, Bhubaneswar-based reporters of national news organizations struggled to find space in national news and justify their salaries. The only time they succeeded was when they reported on alleged starvation deaths: so many have died here, so many have died there, which would be lapped up as headline news. Every now and then, such stories would erupt, and the nation would be outraged.

As long as J.B. Patnaik was chief minister – for some fourteen years in different spells – he made a career out of denying those deaths as fake news. But once out of power, he seized upon them in an attempt to turn the tables on Naveen Patnaik. The Bhubaneswar-based media helped him in great measure, going to town with more reports of starvation deaths. A farmer in Odisha's Rayagada district hired some locals to work on his farm against wages and a meal. Those who ate the meal died. Those who didn't – including the farmer's son who had been at school – survived. It was a clear case of food poisoning, but that didn't deter the media from portraying it as a case of hunger deaths.[13] A lady who was employed in an Anganwadi centre and helped cook meals died. The media alleged starvation death, ignoring the fact that someone preparing food couldn't possibly die of hunger herself.

The reports shook the country and regularly rocked parliament, including when newspapers and television channels alleged that people in the state's hinterland were being forced to eat mango kernels in the absence of food. One bureaucrat raised a pertinent point, asking who ate the mangoes? But logic found little space in the chorus of outrage that swept the nation.

That Odisha was poor and deprivation stalked its people was never in doubt. But the examples of hunger deaths highlighted were clearly ill-researched and possibly wrong. With almost every newspaper awash with such reports, it was not long before I came under pressure from *India Today* editors. They thought I was slipping up and not doing enough. So, it prompted me to take a closer look at the reports and minutely check their veracity. And the story that I finally did was no less startling.

As against the claim that dozens had died in a village, it was found that no more than four people had died. A series of stories done by a national daily on a poor family selling two children for Rs 500 out of desperation also turned out to be incorrect. It transpired the orphaned children were handed over to the reporter as their uncle sought to dispossess them of the house and the Rs 17,000 they had in the local cooperative bank. It was more greed and less despair.

My story in *India Today* – 'Starved of Truth'[14] – citing names of the media houses and their reports hit where it hurt the most. Prime Minister A.B. Vajpayee cited it to shut up critics such as Congress chief Sonia Gandhi on the floor of the House, while local journalists were livid with rage. They bayed for my blood even as journalists in several districts staged noisy demonstrations denouncing the *India Today* story. They made bonfires of the magazine while I was condemned as someone who was insensitive to the harsh reality. A widely circulated local Odia daily, in fact, went a step further. In an opinion piece, it argued that anyone hit and killed by a passing vehicle in the underdeveloped regions of the state ought to be considered a victim of hunger death. Hunger and malnutrition, the paper alleged, had made them unable to cross the road fast enough.

The arguments made were bizarre, but they did little to lessen the heat I faced. The local media had irrevocably turned hostile, and I no longer felt physically safe to attend press conferences.

Having made myself so unwelcome, I looked for a way out, and it came shortly afterwards in the shape of a long-distance phone call from Doha in Qatar. Al Jazeera – the Arabic television channel that had built up quite a notoriety for airing tapes of the fugitive al-Qaeda chief Osama Bin Laden – was interested in hiring me. The channel was planning to launch an English arm, starting with an English website, and its managing editor – an American-Lebanese currently married to a British pop star – was on the line.

I was taken aback. I had not applied for the job and initially suspected that it was a case of mistaken identity. They must have called me by mistake, having got the wrong number, I told myself the first time the phone rang as I drove back home for lunch one day. But Joanne Tucker insisted it was me she wanted to hire. More calls followed. It later turned out that an old friend who had spent some time in the region had recommended me on being asked by an Arab sheikh involved with Al Jazeera.

Things moved quickly as I found out more about the channel and the region – beginning with buying an atlas to locate where exactly Doha and Qatar were on the world map. Soon, I was on my way to join the international channel, escaping a hostile work environment back home. A much larger world awaited me, and I was more than willing to embrace the challenges in store.

4

HELLO HABIBI

'Joining al-Qaeda?' My father's friend sounded more than alarmed when he called as I prepared to pack and leave for Doha to join Al Jazeera. The father's friend was more like family and knew that I had been a kind of a problem child, prompting my parents to seek his counsel on more than one occasion in the past. Now, decades later, he feared he had more reasons to worry.

It was early 2003, and the drumbeats of war could be clearly heard across the world. The United States, fresh from what it felt was its resounding success in uprooting al-Qaeda by invading Afghanistan and toppling the ruling Taliban, was now in the final stages of invading Iraq to unseat its long-time ruler, Saddam Hussein. Separated by some 1,400 km from Iraq, I was set to fly into Doha at a time when the region was rapidly slipping into anarchic turmoil.

American troops were amassing in very large numbers in nearby countries – including in Doha, which was home to the US Central Command – when I arrived to take up my new job. Not many were convinced about my move. *Al* in Arabic is equivalent to 'the' in English, and to have Arabic names for shops and establishments beginning with Al is common. Qatar, with Doha as capital, is a peninsula, and in Arabic, Al Jazeera means 'The Peninsula'. Few in India knew anything about the nuances, and they derived from the channel's name whatever they wished to. That was the case with my father's friend. Ditto with my mother. That Al Jazeera sounded somewhat similar to al-Qaeda was enough reason for her to be worried about my well-being.

For its part, the international channel headquartered in the laidback but prosperous Qatari capital had raised hackles around the globe. It was an Arabic channel then and its aggressive reporting on the region, mostly ruled by despots and marked by lack of personal freedoms, was path-breaking. Countries in its neighbourhood resented it and would routinely ban it from being beamed within their respective borders. But the more the channel was hated, the more its popularity grew on the streets of the Arab world, and now it planned to launch its English arm – first a news website and then a full-fledged TV channel in English. I was among the first batch to arrive for its proposed foray into English.

Since the daring 9/11 attacks, Osama Bin Laden had been on the run, reportedly holed up in Afghanistan. The Americans demanded that the Taliban, ruling the country, hand him over to them. They refused, and the US invaded the country. But Bin Laden gave the American troops the slip and for some ten years – until he was eventually found and killed in the Pakistani garrison town of Abbottabad – no one seemed to know where he was hiding.

But Al Jazeera seemed to know. Every now and then, long before I arrived in Doha, Bin Laden would give exclusive interviews to Al Jazeera from his hideout. Either Al Jazeera reporters would go to meet him, or he would send his pre-recorded tapes. Whatever the case, Al Jazeera's visibility – more appropriately its notoriety – skyrocketed with the airing of the Bin Laden interviews. People with little understanding of the local dynamics and how the region worked mistook the channel as an extension of the terrorist network of al-Qaeda. They were grossly wrong.[1]

The real story is that Qatar is an extremely tiny country that has always felt threatened by its big neighbours like Saudi Arabia. Though rich – with massive reserves of oil and gas – it was never considered to be influential enough and was invariably bullied by its bigger neighbours. Ruled by an enterprising monarch – locally called the Emir – it saw an opportunity to increase its influence when Saudi Arabia backed out of a television channel that it had co-started with the BBC in the mid-1990s. The nascent channel's reporting tested the limits of what the conservative Saudis could tolerate, and the partnership broke down. Suddenly, many Arabic journalists, suitably trained, were unemployed and available for employment.

The enterprising Qatari Emir who had unseated his father in a coup of sorts[2] to come to power seized the opportunity, hired the jobless journalists and launched Al Jazeera. He was way ahead of his time in realizing that he who controlled information would ultimately command influence. Al Jazeera became successful, and as its owner – the channel is bankrolled by the Qatari government – Qatar's importance grew manifold. It was no longer a pushover in a region dominated mostly by despots ruling large countries, and the Qatari Emir found a place at the high table at global meets to discuss regional developments.

None of the decision-makers, both in the West and also in West Asia, liked Al Jazeera. Yet, they couldn't do away with it. The more Al Jazeera's fame roiled the leaders – the then US president George Bush was widely reported to have discussed with British Prime Minister Tony Blair plans to bomb the channel's headquarters[3] – the more it grew in popularity. I often wondered why Bin Laden chose to give his interviews to Al Jazeera and no one else. I got the answer once I reported for duty. The logic was plain and simple: take, for example, Lalu Prasad Yadav, the once-powerful satrap of Bihar. His constituents were predominantly Hindi-speaking, and it made more sense for him to address them through Hindi TV channels such as Aaj Tak or Zee News. Giving interviews to BBC or CNN might have been more prestigious but of little consequence. The same logic possibly weighed in with Bin Laden. The supposed 'jihad' he waged was intended for Arabs, and Al Jazeera was the biggest Arabic channel with unparalleled reach. He, therefore, gave interviews to it.

Whatever the reason, Al Jazeera was controversial and was caught in the middle of escalating uncertainty over the invasion of Iraq. Its reporting reflected the mood on the ground, making it abundantly clear that few people in the region believed the Western spin that Saddam Hussein was being toppled because he possessed weapons of mass destruction. No such weapons were ever found.

Joining Al Jazeera opened up a whole new perspective for me. As the US struck Iraq, we hastily put up an English news website that gave a counterpoint. Iraqis died in the thousands, and supporters of the war celebrated. But in the Al Jazeera newsroom with people drawn from various nationalities, including Iraqis – we called it a mini-United Nations – there were whoops of joy as and when reports of American casualties trickled in. The region, and also the channel, were convinced that the war was wrong and the Iraqi resistance justified.

The point of view that Al Jazeera offered had me hooked, though adjusting to the new workplace was hard. It was a different world altogether, far removed from my comfort zone in Bhubaneswar – my last posting before I left the country's shores. It brought me down to earth by several notches. While in Odisha, I could walk in to meet the chief minister and also socialize with those considered influential. But in Doha, I quickly realized that my immediate past did not count. My new colleagues had not heard of Odisha. They knew about Kolkata, my place of birth, but only vaguely as the city that was home to the iconic Mother Teresa.

The ignorance, it turned out, cut both ways. I, too, seemed to know very little about what my new colleagues knew or were interested in. Just days after I joined, the newsroom went into a tizzy after news broke that a coup was under way in Guinea-Bissau. It was big breaking news, and everyone went to work while I sheepishly googled to find out where the country was. Around the same time, the channel devoted a lot of time and energy to cover a speech by Hasan Nasrallah about the Naqba. I knew nothing about both – the powerful chief of the Lebanon-based armed group Hezbollah or the anniversary marking the exodus of Palestinians from their homeland on Israel being born.

Al Jazeera afforded me an avenue to learn and expand my worldview. It also gave me the opportunity to write for *Outlook* for the first time. The Iraq war had just begun, and the magazine with Vinod Mehta still as its editor was looking for someone residing in the region to write on the situation with a different perspective. A senior member of the editorial staff got in touch with me, and I enthusiastically wrote what I had got to know about the ill-conceived war. My column in the next issue of *Outlook* read:

> One particular Iraqi friend of mine showcases the prevailing mood the best. Genial and soft-spoken, he's enraged the moment western television channels start parroting their lines … his pride hurt, he regains composure only when the customary references are made to fierce Iraqi resistance. "See friend, Iraqis are standing up", he presses my hands tightly, gesturing he has found some peace at least within the overwhelming despair.
>
> It's perhaps only from my vantage position in Doha that I could have seen through the duplicity and double standards and, to be honest, I am seeing them by the dozen, day after day, as the war unfolds. A man is ordinarily presumed to be alive unless proven dead. But in Saddam's case, the western media has presumed him to be dead unless proven alive – ever since US military officials craftily floated news of his death in the very first rush of missile strikes … Though not rage, I have distinct disgust welling up inside me. From it hopefully springs the urge to swim against the tide and let one's voice be heard. Al Jazeera has precisely been doing that and I seem to have landed up at the correct address.[4]

My tryst with *Outlook* began thus, though I had little premonition at that point that I would work for the magazine full-time later. For the time being, my sight was squarely fixed on the immediate, and there was plenty to be busy with. Al Jazeera's English website grew in size and reach, and a couple of years later, an English version of the television channel also came into being. It became an international phenomenon and employees like me prospered, both in terms of perspective and comfort.

Life in Qatar – the second richest country after Luxembourg in terms of per capita income – was predictable and congenial. Tax-free income ensured a good quality of life with big four-wheel drive cars and a luxurious house, sprinkled with occasional holidays in Europe and elsewhere. It got even better when the benevolent Emir came calling. Al Jazeera launched a new studio, and the monarch was pleased on inaugurating it. He announced a full month's extra pay to all staff. He visited again, and this time, he ordered Kahramaa – the government department for electricity and water – not to bill Al Jazeera employees. The largesse seemed limitless, best illustrated by the weighty gold coin I received on completion of five years of service with the channel. There was a function the previous night to felicitate long-serving employees, and I had skipped it. But the next day, as I walked into the office, an Arab colleague accosted me. 'Hello Habibi (my friend), come, come'; he dragged me to his cubicle, opened his drawer and handed me the coin that he said I had earned for my loyalty. I couldn't disagree.

A seat at the state-of-the-art global headquarters of Al Jazeera – a 24/7 channel truly covering the world – allowed us a ringside view of international events. Initially, it intimidated me, so much so that there were one or two nights when I silently wept in the hotel room where I had been put up on arrival. Coming straight from Bhubaneswar, I wasn't prepared for what was in store – beginning with the big swanky limousine that was sent to the airport to pick me up.

On the first night, there was a big office party on the top deck of the upscale Ritz Carlton hotel, and what I saw and heard there had me unnerved. The colleagues I met were from the United States, United Kingdom, Australia, Iraq, Morocco... Some of them had joined days or weeks earlier, and they spoke animatedly about stories they were doing and sources they were speaking to. I've got to rush back to call the Pentagon, said one. Another talked about reaching out to the White House for a quote. The more I listened in, the more I was overwhelmed with fear. Accustomed to calling up state ministers and MLAs mostly, I was close to a nervous meltdown.

As the days, weeks and months passed, the initial jitters dissipated. I began to revel in the raw energy and excitement that swept the Al Jazeera headquarters, and there was hardly a dull moment. We constantly scrambled to cover news, from Mali to Morocco and Gaza to Guatemala. None covered Western Asia and Africa more extensively and in-depth than the channel that had built an enormous network of reporters across these regions. Whatever the time of the day, we were required to be on the top of news that broke anywhere in the world.

'To Give Voice to the Voiceless' was Al Jazeera's tagline and its journalists strived hard to live up to that motto – often taking huge risks, including to their own lives. Tareq Ayyoub was Al Jazeera's reporter in Baghdad when the Iraq war began. The TV cameras were already trained on him as he prepared to go live in the morning of 8 April 2003, with the latest updates on the terrace of the Baghdad office. It was highly risky to report such a bloody conflict even though Ayyoub wore a helmet and a bulletproof jacket as a precaution. TV footage picked up an American tank in the distant background turning its turret towards Ayyoub and firing. Within seconds, Ayyoub was dead.[5]

The mindless killing was outrageous. Martyred in the line of duty, Ayyoub left behind a disconsolate family, including a baby. But being subjected to outrages wasn't entirely uncommon for Al Jazeera journalists. They faced them at regular intervals, at various theatres of conflict across different time zones. Sami al-Hajj was an Al Jazeera cameraman who was covering the US invasion of Afghanistan when he was picked up by security forces sometime in 2001. He was handed over to the Americans who held him first at their detention facility in Kabul's Bagram airfield and then had him transported to Guantanamo Bay.

Sami was imprisoned there until 2008 – mistreated and tortured at the notorious prison the US administration had set up to hold suspected terrorists, minus judicial oversight. Al Jazeera ran a spirited campaign, demanding that Sami be freed. When he was finally released, he returned to Doha to a hero's welcome. The Qatari government rewarded him with Qatari citizenship.

Al Jazeera journalists continued to run into regular trouble. Its reporters – including Australian Peter Greste – found themselves in prison for varying periods of time in Egypt and elsewhere.[6] Security and safety of Al Jazeera staff was constantly a concern, and I had a close shave when for weeks, I stalled the deployment of a spunky Iranian-American reporter to cover the conflict in Syria. My job would have been on the line had I acquiesced.

Dorothy Parvaz was a reporter with the online team, and she repeatedly came up to me, requesting that she be sent to Syria, where an armed uprising against the regime of President Bashar al-Assad had triggered a civil war. For much of my stint with Al Jazeera, I deputed for the digital chief as and when he was away. I was in charge when Dorothy kept pestering me, and I kept saying no. She was a veteran of covering conflicts and had undergone the mandatory hostile environment training that all reporters must complete before being deployed to cover strife. But the dual nature of her nationality – Iranian-American – set my alarm bells ringing. Assad's regime was backed by Tehran, and the US was ranged against the two. To send Dorothy – an American, who Tehran would most likely view as an Iranian dissident or a CIA spy – seemed to be a risky proposition, and I kept saying no.

Not one to give up, the stubborn Dorothy finally had her way when the digital head returned. She flew off, only to disappear moments after she arrived in Syria. What followed were weeks of anxious waiting. There was no news of her, and Al Jazeera launched a worldwide 'Free Dorothy Parvaz' campaign.[7] As was always the case during such situations, back-channel communications were activated, and even the Qatari government chipped in with trying to figure out what happened to Dorothy. She was finally located in a prison in Iran, where she had landed up after being detained by Syrian forces who handed her over to the Iranian army. Diplomatic negotiations secured her release, and Dorothy returned safely. We all were relieved at her release, but I think I gave her the tightest hug when she reported for duty again.

It is a different matter that Dorothy turned into one of my biggest detractors as I grew in stature as one of the senior-most editors in the organization. There was, however, no denying that we did some phenomenally good work as a team. Success in the digital space was all about fastest-finger first, backed by in-depth, incisive content that gave readers information not available elsewhere in the quickest possible time.

We were at the top of our game when the Arab Spring began, starting with the flight of Zine El Abidine Ben Ali, Tunisia's long-time despotic ruler. As his plane took him into exile – our rolling coverage began in right earnest. Ditto was the case every time the Israelis bombed Palestinian territories and chose to raid Gaza. Al Jazeera had reporters on the ground, and the perspective they provided were cutting-edge. At times, fast-paced developments caught us unprepared – as was the case when the then US President Barack Obama announced the capture and killing of Osama Bin Laden in a raid by special forces deep inside Pakistan. It was dawn in Doha – perhaps 5 a.m. – and I was in charge of the news desk. We worked overtime to catch up.

Most of the time, though, careful advance planning saved the day. As it did when the long-ailing Nelson Mandela died. It was nearly midnight, and I was home when frantic calls came from the office, and I rushed to execute with precision what we had planned. Or, when Muammar Gaddafi, the Libyan dictator, was captured and killed following months of bloody conflict. Gaddafi had been on the run with speculation rife he could be hiding somewhere in his stronghold of Sirte. With US forces relentlessly bombing his forces, there was no doubt that it was endgame for Gaddafi. I decided there could only be two possibilities: either he is captured or is killed. I had plans ready for both. As expected, one day in October 2011, news first broke that he had been captured; promptly we went live with all that had been kept ready for such an eventuality. An hour or so later, news came that he had been killed. We were ready for that too.

The tireless and productive work we did together forged friendships and long-lasting relationships. I am certain that if I were to stand in London's Piccadilly Circus for a few hours, I would run into some old colleagues who had gone back to their country having served time in Doha. There were so many of them. And among the many friendships that I came to cherish, one is the bonding that I still enjoy with an ex-colleague from Morocco. The others I continue to be in touch with are from Iraq, Egypt, Canada and Malaysia. Al Jazeera opened the windows of the world to me.

Not everything at Al Jazeera was rosy, and there were plenty of reasons to rue as well. Though it claimed to practice fearless journalism, its fearlessness deserted it when it came to covering what happened inside Qatar. A Qatari poet was jailed for a poem criticizing the Emir, and the channel barely reported it even when it vociferously took up the cases of activists around the globe who experienced similar harassment. A big fire in a shopping mall owned by a powerful sheikh claimed many lives, and no accountability was fixed. Al Jazeera did not follow up on what happened as consistently as it would normally have done if such a thing had happened elsewhere.

Its obvious double standards touched new depths when the Egyptian deep state launched its campaign to unseat the Muslim Brotherhood government headed by Mohamed Morsi. Always supposed to be a supporter of political Islam and the Brotherhood, a newsreader read out the news of gunshots being fired from inside a mosque in Cairo where Brotherhood members were sheltered. That was a narrative that the channel didn't want to highlight during the crackdown for which it held the Egyptian army clearly as the aggressor. So, what the newsreader read out before slipping into a short commercial break horrified many at the channel. When the news resumed, the newsreader had been mysteriously changed.

Plagued by factions, as is the case with big organizations, petty politicking ran amuck with each group plugging its own agenda. Al Jazeera English broadcast content that was slick and sophisticated, ideal for the Western world. Al Jazeera Arabic was relatively less so and more straightforward. Al Jazeera Mubasher that telecast conferences and events live was more rabid and rabble-rousing. Thus, Al Jazeera was pulled in different directions but powered by deep pockets. I got unwittingly caught in the crossfire. As a Hindu and an Indian, I stood no chance when targeted by an unsympathetic boss and some conservative colleagues.

Al Jazeera's coverage of Kashmir that they considered no less than occupied by Indian forces was increasingly becoming shrill. The rise of Narendra Modi – described as the 'Butcher of Gujarat[8]' by some[9,10] – also caused a lot of heartburn among the largely Muslim staff, and my calls for balance and objectivity were misinterpreted. I vainly fought to have well-rounded coverage with voices from both sides represented. I came to be increasingly viewed as a closet RSS sympathiser, and my stint in Doha ended in due course.

Returning to India, I found myself waiting at the reception of *Outlook*'s Delhi office, hoping for an audience with the then editor. If not a regular job, I needed an engagement to keep myself busy, and I pitched the proposal that I be a stringer for the magazine from Odisha, where I planned to settle down. I was clearly counting on the house that I retained and the many friends I had in the state.

Though I was meeting the editor in person for the first time, he was extremely generous. He knew me from my bylines and readily agreed. Yes, as and when you reach Bhubaneswar, you can start, he graciously said. But, as has been a pattern with most of my professional career, it was not to be. Jobs normally never seemed to materialize for me the first time round. It required multiple attempts, and keeping with the time-tested trend, my time at *Outlook* was destined to wait. *Hindustan Times* wanted me instead.

You may call it a remarkable coincidence, but the job with *Hindustan Times* finally fructified after what was possibly the fourth attempt. Sometime in 2010-11, I had messaged the then editor Samar Halarnkar – a former *India Today* colleague – more out of curiosity to see if I still retained market value in India from where I had been absent for so long. The next morning when I woke up, I was surprised to see several messages from one Rajesh Mahapatra, who I knew was in a senior position at *HT* but did not know personally. We spoke on the phone, and Rajesh wanted me to visit Delhi immediately.

In India on vacation, I came over to the capital the next day, and we hit it off instantly. Rajesh, who was from Odisha, was apparently aware of my reporting for *India Today* during my time in the state and we went to meet Samar together. He seemed to have a favourable opinion of me, and they excitedly told me their plans to start an edition in Bengaluru, their first in south India. Pleased with what I had heard, I was encouraged to make plans for my return.

The preliminary talks over, I went back to Doha and waited to hear from them. But it was not to be. Samar left rather abruptly – *HT* editorship had a reputation for being a game of musical chairs – and another media veteran, Sanjoy Narayan, took his place. Some months later, it was Sanjoy's turn to call me. Come to Delhi, he said. *HT* sent my flight tickets and I showed up in Sanjoy's room. 'How have you been? We are meeting after a long time', he said, welcoming me. I was taken aback. Sanjoy had earlier worked with *Business Today* – the business magazine from the India Today group – but I couldn't recall ever meeting him. I played along, though, and the two of us talked in greater detail about the Bengaluru plan. 'It is not us deciding, but you deciding when you will join', I was told.

I was excited. I had grown somewhat tired of the anonymity of my Al Jazeera job and wished to be back in the hurly-burly of Indian journalism. My hope to regain what I had voluntarily given up for gathering international experience and earning some honest, tax-free money was rekindled. I waited for the next call, which mysteriously never came. *HT*, I later learnt, had jettisoned its south India plans. They called up some two years later while I was holidaying in Sri Lanka. Rajesh again wanted to see me, and I hurriedly made my way to Delhi. This time, the editors were exploring if I might be interested in taking over either their Bhopal or Lucknow editions. More talks and calls followed before the trail went cold again.

In 2015, I was finally leaving Al Jazeera and weighed in my options to stay engaged on my return to India. I messaged several people – from *Outlook*'s editor Krishna Prasad to *India Today*'s Aroon Purie. I also texted Rajesh. Some three days later, he returned the call. This time, on the table was the position of National Affairs Editor that *HT* wished to create for overseeing its network of reporters outside Delhi and across the states. Talks progressed, but at a snail's pace. Nevertheless, I found myself in Sanjoy's room at the *HT* headquarters in Delhi's KG Marg some months later. 'No one knows you better in this building than I. The job is yours,' he said. It meant keeping at abeyance the offer to work for *Outlook*, at least for a few more years.

I came to live in Delhi for the first time in my life, uncertain about whether I had it in me to live up to the responsibility that *HT* had entrusted me with. Besides being a stranger to the city, I had zero experience in reporting from many crucial states such as Uttar Pradesh, Kashmir or, say, Punjab. Forget reporting; I had never even visited them. I silently nursed my self-doubt as I made my way to the *HT* office. I was in for a shock. The elevator at the end of the ground floor foyer was ready with its door wide open, but just as I was about to step in, I was stopped.

Security guards talking over walkie-talkies curtly told me I would have to wait since *HT* chairperson Sobhana Bhartia was about to arrive. When she arrived to the sound of whistles that the security staff blew incessantly, she went up on the elevator alone as a dozen people stood by downstairs awaiting their turn. I later learnt that reserving the elevator as and when the chairperson arrived or left, no matter how many people were waiting in the busy building, was standard practice. I realized feudalism was alive and kicking in the country where I had just returned.

What lay ahead on the editorial floors of *HT* was even more traumatic. I found myself at sea, unable to make any sense of the various operational layers that existed. I was the national affairs editor, and it was clear that the state correspondents, say, in Kerala or Tamil Nadu, where the paper had no edition, were directly under my control. The problem was with the bureaus attached to various publication centres, such as Mumbai, Chandigarh, Kolkata and Lucknow. The reporters there reported to their respective resident editors, and I simply did not know how to bring them under my wing. I sent out messages, asking for stories that I wished them to do, and came up against resistance. One resident editor – who again I knew from my *India Today* days – called late in the night, apparently sozzled. He resented what he saw as my interference and raised his voice. Given our past relationship, it took me time to realize he was serious when he said he would 'screw' my happiness. When I realized this, I knew I had hit a roadblock.

On their part, the editors in Delhi tried to empower me. Reporters from across the country were flown in for a day-long meeting with me. But I still failed to find my feet. The incident at Dadri on 28 September 2015 – where a Muslim man, Mohammed Akhlaq, was beaten to death on the suspicion of possessing beef [11]– happened, and it blew up into a major story. But I didn't know that Dadri was just an hour away from Delhi. For that matter, I didn't even know at that point what National Capital Region (NCR) was, or that Gurgaon, adjacent to Delhi, was in Haryana.

Under the impression that Dadri was in UP and, therefore, the responsibility of the Lucknow edition, I let the story be handled by them. But the immediate coverage was far from spectacular. UP reporters did not focus on Dadri since it was closer to Delhi. Delhi reporters, too, did not cover it extensively as it was technically in UP. As the bridge in optimizing our reporting resources, I had failed badly in my first test.

The pressure was on me, and my honeymoon at *HT* was extremely short-lived. Some two weeks into the job, a goof-up happened in the national pages of the newspaper and Sanjoy was livid. My job wasn't to make the pages. As a matter of fact, I was not even supposed to be in the office when the desk made the pages late at night. But the next morning, I got called into Sanjoy's room and got the dressing down of my life. 'Hiring you has been one big mistake', he angrily proclaimed, dismissing me from the room. I muttered if I could come back and explain myself later, but Sanjoy would have none of it. 'I have no time', he said.

I was in a state of shock over what Sanjoy told me, as well as the manner in which the edit meetings were conducted at *HT*. We had at least three of them, beginning with a conference call at

10.30 a.m., following which we rushed to the office for another meeting at 12.30 p.m. The next and final meeting happened in the crammed conference room at 5.30 p.m. I dreaded attending them as they were borderline abusive. Senior editors were routinely called names – donkeys, monkeys and what not – and I silently suffered from a culture shock. *HT* seemed insufferable, and I told my wife not to unpack all our belongings that had arrived by ship from Doha. This job could be cut short anytime, I warned her.

Fortunately, though, some senior editors – among them Nic Dawes, the South African chief content officer of *HT*, and Rajesh – helped me tide over the testing times. They were patient with me, and I gradually got into a rhythm. I began to understand how *HT* worked and how to navigate the myriad layers of authority that hobbled the organization. Over a period of time, the national affairs team came to carry clout. Deputies were drafted to strengthen my hand, and a special team of reporters was created who we could parachute to anywhere in the country as and when the situation demanded. Not everyone was pleased with our growing influence, but with senior management covering my back, people fell in line. States' coverage in *HT* began to sparkle in no time.

HT already had an excellent pool of reporters; all that was needed was to motivate and mentor them a bit. Once a story idea was pitched and finalized, the reporters were ever ready to deliver. Special stories that they churned out started to dominate the paper as we together as a team set a scorching pace. There were many stories that stood out. After some months, Sanjoy – who had provided the paper a degree of stability – quit after being at the helm for about eight years. Bobby Ghosh – my old friend from my Visakhapatnam days as a rookie reporter – came in as the next chief editor. It meant there was no let-up in the stand-out stories that the national team churned out daily without fail.

There were many that I can recall. Ritesh Mishra, for one, was a young intrepid reporter whom we had shifted from Bhopal to Raipur in Chhattisgarh. One day, he called excitedly to inform me that the newsreader of a local cable television channel had earlier in the day read out the news of her husband's death in a road accident. He was unsure whether a local story made for national news. I jumped, and the moment he provided me with all the details – names of the newsreader and the channel and the chronology of events – I quickly wrote out a report and gave it online. Our traffic instantly spiked, and the unparalleled act of composure and courage became a global story.[12] It was on the front pages of almost every paper the next day, with the venerable *Time* magazine following up.

Ritesh never ceased to surprise with the stories he came up with regularly. He found in the national affairs team a perfect ally who appreciated what he did, and he hit the front pages often. Including when he reported on an IPS officer of the state who once was a doctor. The officer had shot a dreaded Maoist in an encounter and when the man lay bleeding profusely, he saved his life by treating him. This story,[13] too, went viral and secured a place on the paper's front pages.

HT turned out to be a haven for enterprising reporters, and we in Delhi simply ensured that their work shone. A Supreme Court judge ruled that the national anthem be mandatorily played at movie theatres, and I sent reporters across the country to watch movies and how the audience reacted. What we found made us laugh. In some theatres, couples cooing in dark corners were forced to stand up. But in Bolpur – the town in West Bengal where Rabindranath Tagore's seat of open learning, Santiniketan, is situated and where the Nobel laureate penned his famous song – the national anthem was not being played. The newsreel of the song was yet to reach where it should have mattered the most.

We tried to be constantly different in the content we produced. A two-paragraph news report in an obscure paper caught my attention: it talked about a jail near Hyderabad that had been converted into a tourist attraction. Apparently, tourists could go there, buy a ticket and spend a day or two in jail wearing prisoners' clothes. I called our Hyderabad reporter Srinivas Apparasu and asked him to check it out. Two days later, *HT*'s front page had a story accompanied with a photograph of Srinivas sitting inside a cell looking every inch a prisoner, narrating his day as an inmate.[14]

We begged, borrowed and stole ideas if needed. Even the smallest of news items tucked away in various papers could find us in hot pursuit of a story. I came across one during a trip to Lucknow, while I gorged on the biryani that our resident editor Sunita Aron invariably laid out for me every time I visited. A newspaper that was lying around caught my attention. A small report in it talked about a young girl in Bareilly, twenty weeks pregnant, seeking an abortion since her rich paramour would not marry her.

We had a very fine reporter, Chandan Kumar, in the town, and he was told to follow up on the girl's travails as she knocked the doors of the judiciary for the requisite permission to abort. Doctors said an abortion at that stage was risky and kept advising against it even as the girl's desperation grew. The courts dragged its feet, forcing the girl to finally deliver a child that she clearly did not want. We kept doing stories on her, and soon other papers followed. Over time, the Bareilly girl was big news and the day she delivered, a horde of parents seeking to adopt the child descended on Bareilly. Some good came out of our sustained coverage. The last time I enquired, the girl's lover had made amends with her.[15]

That our journalism made a difference thrilled us, and we chased stories that cried out to be told with empathy and single-minded devotion. An underaged schoolgirl in Rajasthan stopped coming to school, and her worried classmates found out that she had been married. The friends approached the local administration and demanded that she be returned. Our crack team of reporters followed suit and did what were indeed memorable stories. The girl returned to school.

One of our young Kashmir reporters, Abhishek Saha, had an uncanny eye for spotting such human interest stories. A young girl in Srinagar lost her eye to pellets that were much in use to quell street protests. Turning blind, she sank into darkness. But Saha was there to document her story the day she returned to school, helped by her friends to overcome her disability.

The stories that came in from the states were of the kind that made people sit up and take note. One such was when an Indian army officer, Major Leetul Gogoi, tied a Kashmiri to the bonnet of his jeep and drove around,[16] claiming he was only holding him as a 'human shield' to escape from a violent crowd. When the news broke with photographs showing a helpless Farooq Ahmad Dar tied to the bonnet, it inevitably ignited a firestorm. It further divided a nation already high on nationalism.[17]

While many were outraged at the plight of the ordinary Kashmiri citizen, many former army officials felt that Gogoi had set a dangerous precedent for terrorists and others ranged against the Indian state who could, hereafter, use the incident as an excuse to ill-treat soldiers they capture in a similar fashion. There were also those who hailed the army major. Gogoi was proclaimed a 'hero' in his hometown in Assam and elsewhere in India. Some in Assam actually went to town, lionizing Gogoi as a modern-day Lachit Borphukan – a medieval war hero who fought the Mughals.

In the fog of confusion marked by claims and counter-claims, it was important to figure out what had exactly happened and the sequence of events. I called up our Srinagar bureau and told them to retrace Gogoi's journey the next day. Begin from where Gogoi started that day, where and when he picked up Dar, tied him to the bonnet, right until he finally set him free. Saha and the other reporter weren't very impressed. What will it prove, they asked. I insisted and, the following day, both of them set out to retrace Gogoi's steps.

As they went along, they spoke to locals and figured out the sequence of events. What emerged was that the major had not really used Dar as a human shield only to escape a crowd. He had him tied up for hours, releasing him only around 4 p.m. – long after he had got out of the mob that had surrounded him around noon. It was important to call out this lie, and *HT*'s front page lead the next day did precisely that.[18] Bobby was the chief editor, and he was in no doubt that it was an important story to do, irrespective of the risks, including being portrayed as 'anti-national'. As it turned out, an army tribunal indicted Major Gogoi a year later over another case involving 'moral turpitude'.[19] As Gogoi turned villain, we felt vindicated. The icing on the cake was when Saha won the prestigious Ramnath Goenka award for his reporting in Kashmir. There was no one who was more thrilled that day than I.

Not all reporters rose to the occasion and measured up to the challenges, though, or accepted my captaincy as national affairs editor. I ran into an unsavoury episode while dealing with a state correspondent. For some reason, he saw me as his adversary and an ally of Union minister Dharmendra Pradhan. It is a different matter that my subsequent book on Naveen Patnaik – an unauthorized biography that hit the stands in 2018 – didn't make Dharmendra very happy because he felt I had unnecessarily idolized the Odisha chief minister as a remarkable phenomenon.

For that matter, the book left readers a bit confused and undecided whether it was pro- or anti-Patnaik. Like everyone else, the chief minister had some great positives alongside several deep character flaws. My book detailed them all and made it neither a eulogy nor a hatchet job. But then the reporter was convinced of my supposed ulterior motives, refused to cooperate and consequently complained to the senior management about me.

Dharmendra was positioning himself as a chief ministerial aspirant, and I wanted our political coverage from Odisha to reflect that. But the reporter wouldn't relent and refused to comply with whatever I said. For some unknown reason, he thought Dharmendra was a nobody who I was hellbent on promoting. Soon, he simply refused to take my calls and orders. It became unpleasant, bitter and stressful, finally resulting in his dismissal. Taking someone's job leaves a bitter taste. It didn't taste any better when I was tasked with handing out pink slips in Bhopal and Indore later.

Life in *Hindustan Times* under Bobby was buzzing and busy. We had already shifted to the swanky, state-of-the-art floor of a recently built newsroom and were in the middle of a frenetic 'digital-first' transformation. It meant ramping up online coverage and its offerings, including podcasts and videos. Stiff deadlines were set, and the pressure to deliver was high. Seemingly an early bird, Bobby had no problem coming to the office early. But many of us struggled and forced ourselves out of bed to reach the office for the first edit meeting of the day scheduled at 9.30 a.m. By then, I would have had to speak to reporters, discuss stories of the day, and present a detailed news plan.

With such a packed day, there was little time to think about anything else. Even so, we soon came face to face with a crisis that posed a moral and ethical dilemma. *HT*, we were told, was under financial stress and operations had to be scaled down. This necessitated cost-cutting, invariably involving shutting down some editions of the paper and letting go of people from other centres. The bloodbath began, as editors pored over Excel sheets to decide who could be sacrificed and who would be retained.

Once decided, some editors were sent to various centres to do the painful culling. Someone went to Kolkata to sack people; another went to Bihar. I was sent to Bhopal and Indore in what I still hold as one of the worst trips I have ever undertaken. Ironically, I checked in at the posh Jehan Numa Palace Hotel of Bhopal for the purpose of pulling the plug on the livelihoods of several colleagues.

The next day, the office staff came in one by one to be told if they were staying or going. Those going were unceremoniously handed the pink slip over small talk. There was little I could say to provide solace. What do you tell a middle-aged photographer who sits before you and weeps inconsolably? 'Sir, I have loans and from tomorrow, when the word goes out that I have no job, the creditors will line up in front of my door. Where will I go?' he said as a stony silence settled in the room.

We would again fall silent some months later when Bobby suddenly broke the news that he had quit. 'The official announcement is on its way,' he said, in what otherwise could have qualified as a rather uneventful day in September 2017. Brought in with much fanfare only about eleven months earlier, he evidently had ruffled a few feathers. His no-nonsense style of journalism was out of sync with a paper like *Hindustan Times*, known to walk the tightrope. The paper had what were widely perceived to be 'holy cows' – people against whom you couldn't write or had to give undue prominence. One was the late Union minister Arun Jaitley. The other was Madhya Pradesh royalty Jyotiraditya Scindia. Every time Scindia – Yuvaraj in local circles – said something, we had to report it. And if stories that still do the rounds in *HT*'s corridors are to be believed, anything unfavourable to the people who mattered couldn't be reported.

It allegedly happened once when Jaitley was contesting the 2014 Lok Sabha elections from Amritsar in Punjab. He faced rough weather and a story appeared in *HT* saying so. A sub-editor who had passed the story was not seen in the office after the story appeared. Grapevine has it she was fired. It is a different matter that Jaitley, in fact, lost the election.

Bobby was pushing the envelope constantly with the objective brand of both-sides journalism that the paper pursued under him. And matters came to a head when he allowed the paper to launch a 'Hate Tracker' series at a time when the country seemed awash with vigilante-style justice over religious beliefs and food habits. Mohammed Akhlaq had been killed in Dadri, Pehlu Khan[20] – a cattle trader – was publicly beaten to death in Rajasthan. There were many such instances and *Hindustan Times*' Hate-Tracker attempted to document every single example of mindless violence that threatened the country's social fabric.

Obviously, the painstaking recording of hate crimes didn't fit into the narrative that those in power wanted to be publicized, and Bobby fell in their bad books. A sugar-coated email landed in our inboxes announcing that Bobby, after a short but glorious stint, had decided to quit, having chosen to move on in his career.

Bobby left, and a very turbulent phase of transition began at *Hindustan Times*. It was at a time when I was preparing to write my book on Naveen Patnaik. I went on two months' leave, but before I left, the new bosses reassured me I would be welcomed back. By the time I returned from my sabbatical, the news floor had drastically changed. Heads had rolled, and people shifted around. I got back to a changed *Hindustan Times* and lasted no more than five days.

On what was to be my last day with the paper, the crack team of reporters who were parachuted everywhere for special stories was taken away from me. None explained why, but I was told they would henceforth report to someone else. Then, there was a sudden meeting where it was announced in the presence of the HR manager that someone – much junior to me in age and experience – was being bumped up and I would hereafter report to him. I got the message. The meeting lasted ten minutes or so, and I took another ten minutes to write out my resignation letter, pick up my bag and leave the *Hindustan Times*.

The *Caravan* magazine some months later devoted its cover story to the goings-on at *Hindustan Times* and had some very interesting details, including the new editor proudly proclaiming to staff that 'to see him at work was as good as witnessing Beethoven compose music'.[21] It set tongues wagging but brought me no cheer, as I sat at home staring at an uncertain future and walking aimlessly around my neighbourhood. Suddenly jobless and minus many friends in the city, I had no place to go.

And then, *Outlook* happened.

5

AN INLOOK

THE DOUBLE-SPREAD ADVERTISEMENT LOOKED AWESOME. IT proudly announced *Outlook*'s marquee annual event, the *Outlook* SpeakOut, to be held in Delhi in two days' time. The theme was 'women empowerment', and it exhorted women to resist any pushback and reclaim the advances they had made in India in the face of deep-rooted patriarchy. Calling on all women to rejoice over the strides they had made, the advertisement also showcased an impressive line-up of speakers – southern film star and politician Khushboo Sundar, actresses Kubbra Sait, Shefali Shah and Kirti Kulhari, Paralympian Deepa Malik and the then Indian Mahila Congress chief, Sushmita Dev, among others. The chief guest was to be the then Union Minister of Women and Child Development and Textiles, and the advertisement had her photograph displayed prominently at the top of the right-hand page. But there was a major problem. Underneath her photograph and above her designation where it should have said 'Smriti Irani', it simply said: SMT. IDIOT – all in caps.

My eyes popped, and my heart skipped several beats as the advertisement was presented to me that Thursday afternoon. It was about two hours after the magazine – on being printed in the wee hours – had reached our office and my desk. I had flipped through the pages, checking all the editorial content, but had not bothered to check the advertisements. In any case, the same advertisement about the *Outlook* event had been carried in at least two previous issues of the magazine without any problem. This time, someone in the editorial team chanced to look at the advertisement and froze. Gathering his thoughts after the initial shock, he came running down to the floor where I sat. He laid open the advertisement in front of me, and I couldn't believe what I saw.

We were stunned and speechless, not knowing how to react. Our own annual event was just two days away, and we, in our advertisement in the latest issue of the magazine, had called the Union minister 'Smt Idiot'. It blanked me out completely for a while. When I came to my senses, I picked up the magazine and ran across to Indranil's room. He was in a meeting, but literally fell off his seat when I showed him the advertisement.

Having spent decades in the media, I knew a thing or two about printers' devils. Mistakes happen – some serious and some that can be brushed off as entertaining. For example, a newspaper in Hyderabad had the practice of stating 'By Our Staff Reporter' underneath the story headline. The headlines were in bigger fonts and 'By Our Staff Reporter' invariably in a much smaller font size. But one day, something went wrong, and both the headline and the credit line for a report on the front page appeared in the same font size. It read: 'Girl raped in city by our staff reporter'.

Such bloopers, though rare, were not entirely uncommon, and I have in my career come across mistakes such as a headline proclaiming, 'Blind student invited to watch Republic Day Parade in Delhi'. Similar mistakes occasionally happened at *Outlook* as well, despite our best efforts to cut them down. Pictures at times would get mixed up and we would carry the photograph of the wrong person. We would get facts, figures and quotes wrong too at times, which we duly corrected by carrying a corrigendum in the following issues.

This one, though, was beyond correction and its potential consequences were huge. After all, it was without any precedent. When have you ever come across an organization publicly deriding its chief guest as an idiot? For a while, a million thoughts raced through our minds. The event on which a lot of money rode, with several sponsors bankrolling it, seemed destined for cancellation. Smriti Irani, we feared, would be livid. Also, *Outlook* would get a terribly bad name. We were certain that the advertisement would fall in the hands of people who would take to social media to amplify it. That a magazine could describe its own chief guest so derogatorily was also a great media story, and we seemed headed for an excruciating bout of bad press. We were mortified by the impending prospect of a PR disaster and a total loss of face.

All of us were shell-shocked, and for a while, a stony silence enveloped the office floor. Then all hell broke loose. I shouted, the CEO shouted, while other members of the staff stood by in utter disbelief. We all wondered how such a mistake could happen, but for the moment, what weighed on our minds the most was how we could save our skins. As was the norm, some seventy copies of the magazine had already been distributed internally within the office. We ordered the office peons to run and fetch all the issues.

Staff in circulation and subscription departments were hurriedly called and sternly instructed to halt the distribution of the issue. What we heard wasn't encouraging. The distribution process was well under way, and bike-borne couriers were already en route to retail stores, at least in Delhi. And the magazine was on its way to different centres across the country. 'Get them, get them. Get back each and every copy', we yelled, prompting ashen-faced staff to shout the order down the command chain. Everyone lost their cool. Tempers rose as panic swept through the office.

The task at hand – to retrieve copies and repair the damage – seemed impossible. I was certain that at least some copies would reach the outside world. What if a staffer had already left the office with a copy? What if even one copy had made it to the stands and then on to the hand of a reader? Sooner or later, the blunder would be noticed and it would go viral. There seemed to be no escape from the public denunciation that would almost certainly follow. I was convinced that I, as *Outlook*'s editor-in-chief, would be caricatured mercilessly. A total loss of face looked inevitable.

Overwhelmed by fear, the frantic rearguard action moved into top gear. Promoters were informed about the mistake and a decision quickly made to destroy the entire issue and print a fresh one. But the first task was to get back all the copies with the damaging advertisement. Bundles of the magazine were making their way to cities and towns by train, and circulation staff were told to take the earliest flights and await their arrival at their respective destinations. They were told to grab them the moment they arrived and burn them. They were required to send photographs of the bonfires being made as proof of the destruction that was to be undertaken on a war footing.

As we raced against time, the office peons returned with some good news. They had managed to get back every copy distributed internally. Surprisingly, no one had left with a copy yet. Certain that some copies would still sneak out, I prepared to inform Smriti Irani. She needed to be prepared for what might follow. But how would I tell her, and what would I tell her, I wondered amid intense trepidation. I was well acquainted with her and knew she had a mercurial temper. I took more than a few deep breaths and tried to muster enough courage before calling her. Her cell was switched off, and I checked with a few sources who told me she was at a campaign rally for the Maharashtra state elections. I left her a message – 'Need to talk to you. It's urgent.' She called back after a while, and what I thought would be one of the most embarrassing conversations of my life began.

Smriti Irani surprisingly turned out to be quite a sport, at least for the time being. 'What, Smt Idiot? Oh! You guys think I am an idiot', she quipped. I told her that we still hadn't figured out how the mistake happened and were desperately trying to get all the printed copies back. But there was every chance some copies might pass into the public domain; I cautioned her. 'In that case, I will file a defamation case for rupees five crore', she said after hearing me out. She didn't sound serious and laughed intermittently. I was relieved. I told her we would be reprinting the issue, and she responded by saying she looked forward to being present at our event on Saturday. I hung up, immensely relieved.

As it turned out, luck was on our side. We miraculously managed to lay our hands on every single copy that had gone out for distribution and the entire edition was promptly pulped. Only one copy of the magazine with that offensive advertisement survives till today – safely tucked in my cupboard at home. We reprinted the entire issue. Two days later, Smriti Irani turned up at the appointed hour at our event, and alighting from the car, the first thing she asked me was, 'Ruben da, now tell me what happened?'

By then, I had all the answers. Our internal investigations showed that a member of our design team had played what she foolishly thought was a prank. The advertisement had been designed and laid out on page weeks before. It had been printed in earlier issues. But just when the current issue was to be sent to press, one of the designers had it opened on his computer and was to send it out again for printing, when he went to the washroom. One of his colleagues – the designer with a prank in mind – came up and changed Smriti Irani's name to 'Smt Idiot'. She quietly went back to work, and the unsuspecting designer, on returning from the washroom, sent the advertisement for printing. What could be described as one of the biggest blunders in printing history was thus scripted. Supposedly just a prank, it endangered the reputation of *Outlook* and threatened to derail its annual event. We'd had a close shave.

Neither the designer nor I got off lightly. She lost her job – summarily dismissed the next day. It came back to haunt me some months later when in the normal course, we reported something on our *Outlook* website against Smriti Irani. It was World Handloom Day and one of our reporters reported that all was not well at the textile ministry. Among everything else, a critic was quoted as saying some unsavoury things against the minister, and she took strong objection.

Her WhatsApp message to me the following day read thus: 'Ethical reportage impresses upon an organisation the responsibility of getting both sides of the story … the fact that *Outlook* ran a one-sided agenda is not surprising. It in fact underlines the reality that the nonsense written about me was not a mistake but a deliberate attempt to bring disrepute and discomfort.' She had clearly not got over the advertisement fiasco and nursed a grudge and cited it the moment she came in for bad press.

I chose to clarify, saying someone had played a prank and lost her job for the advertisement. As for the story on the textile ministry, officials had been quoted. However, I offered that we were willing to interview her to set the record straight. But she would have none of it. 'Not needed. Thanks', she responded. Having regularly attended our events and even written articles for us, my working relationship with the minister abruptly ended.

The fracas over the advertisement encapsulated in more ways than one my rather eventful stint as *Outlook*'s editor. There was never a dull day, though it was not always as dramatic as the day we discovered the advertisement goof-up. Plucked out of what could be best described as virtual anonymity – I was more of a backroom boy at *Hindustan Times* having returned to the country after a long absence of more than twelve years – I wasn't the expected choice for the job that had grown in stature because of the legendary Vinod Mehta. Many, including *Outlook* staffers, were surprised when my name was announced. They possibly anticipated someone better known in local circles to be their editor.

Though I had confidence in my own abilities as a journalist, I was little known in Delhi. I had never worked in the city as a reporter, and my circle of acquaintances here was limited. Everyone thought that people with a greater degree of acceptance and relative fame stood a better chance. Nripendra Misra, the secretary to Prime Minister Modi and possibly the most powerful bureaucrat in the country then gave adequate hints of how coveted the job was when I met him for a formal chat on becoming the editor. I had sought an appointment and went to meet him at the PMO. It was evident that Misra had done his background check on me. He received me warmly, and we had a friendly conversation. Before I left, he told me he was glad I had got the job on my own merit. 'At least four senior journalists had their eyes on your position and sought our recommendations', the elderly official said with a mischievous smile.

Already happy with my new job, what Misra said made me happier still. Having spent several months sitting idle – at home or roadside tea stalls not too long ago – there now was a spring in my step. There was a huge sense of relief, too, as my gamble to abruptly walk out of *Hindustan Times* had paid off. I did initially nurse some doubts about the correctness of my decision to quit. But the unpleasant stories that kept trickling out of KG Marg and my *Outlook* editorship helped to convince me that I had done the right thing.

The expectations that my new job carried were high, but the most daunting of the tasks was to earn the respect of the *Outlook* staff. Not knowing much about me, many of them seemed to have concluded that I lacked the intellectual bandwidth to be their editor. The day I walked into the job for the first time, I knew what lay ahead. Chastised adequately after having witnessed the rough transition at my previous job, I struck a conciliatory tone at the very first town hall meet that I chaired some two hours after reporting for duty.

Some unsavoury stories had already filtered through to me – including one about an earlier editor who preferred to be disconcertingly aloof. But for a few chosen ones, who evidently were part of his select coterie, none could meet him easily. Not even the editor's secretary, who sat right outside his cabin. Staff who wished to meet had to send an email to the secretary, who then passed it on to the editor. The editor, if he chose to, wrote back to the secretary giving a time, which then would be relayed back to the staff. The meeting happened thereafter. There were other stories as well, such as one previous editor briefing reporters about the reports he wanted to be done. People to be spoken to were suggested, as also the slant the story should ultimately take. But often, when the reporters went out to report on the story, what they found on the ground were different from what was originally sought. The stories were invariably spiked.

At my first meeting, I made it a point to reach out to one and all. I only voiced respect. I took care to tell the staff – particularly the senior ones – that I respected the work they did and nothing will be done to undermine them. Yes, some new talent may be brought in, but that would only be to strategically strengthen the team, not to undercut anyone. That calmed the anxieties that some perhaps experienced. I then purposefully made light of my academic qualifications and the supposed lack of intellectual bandwidth. I had never been under any illusions of ever being a meritorious student. I studied as much as was required to pass examinations, and I had a simple graduation degree under my belt. I said so to the staff in a somewhat lighter vein, and everyone laughed.

The ice was quickly broken, and we moved on to discussing story ideas for subsequent issues. I took care that it stayed that way, and there was an atmosphere of camaraderie. I kept my door open, and anyone could walk in anytime they wanted. Small gestures mattered and when, the next day, we all went for lunch together, I asked my office driver to join us at the table, which was noticed.

What got noticed more was my first decisive act at the end of my first week. I found that while I was the editor, I had two deputies. One was the deputy managing editor and the other was the deputy executive editor. They had been in the roles of deputies for several years. I got them promoted, making them full-fledged managing editor and executive editor. It sent out a message that I wasn't threatened by anyone and was happy to see the staff grow in stature.

Building bridges with the team was the easier part. Far more difficult turned out to be coming out of the shadow of *Outlook*'s past. Vinod Mehta's legacy loomed large, and much of our magazine's reputation rested on the goodwill he enjoyed even years after his demise. Wherever I went and whoever I met, they always told me about Mehta and how good he was. I didn't hate the compliments reserved for *Outlook*'s founding editor. On the contrary, I viewed it as a great asset that we needed to leverage for the benefit of the organization.

Besides putting up his framed photograph in my room, I let it be known to all those who cared to listen that I genuinely respected Vinod Mehta. That included Sumita, Mehta's wife. A very fine lady with tremendous grace and poise; I told her when we met that she could continue to count on *Outlook* as part of her family. Mine were possibly just empty words, but Sumita lived up to the warmth she displayed for me. She happened to be one of the two signatories who recommended my application for membership to Delhi's India International Centre (IIC). She, in fact, arranged for the other one too.

Yet, not everything about *Outlook*'s past was to be proud about, and some of these aspects haunted me as an editor for a long time. For one, Vinod Mehta, despite his extraordinary journalistic credentials, was seen by many to be a supporter of the Congress. It gave *Outlook* the cast of being a 'Congress magazine', an image I struggled to shed. I felt no affinity for any particular political party and preferred to be neutral in the manner I conducted myself as an editor. Even so, the stigma stayed, posing infinite challenges. The top leadership of the BJP eyed us with suspicion, made worse by the impression that we were also part of the 'left-liberal Lutyens' clique', whom they disliked.

To steer clear of stereotypes was a tall task. I came up against one with the Aam Aadmi Party. Delhi was headed for elections in 2020, and I was naturally keen that we be the first to interview the party supremo, Arvind Kejriwal. Kejriwal had not been giving interviews for some time, and we realized it could be a kind of a coup if we could get him to talk to us. There were many things to ask – from the allegation that the AAP was a 'B-team of the BJP' to being a closet proponent of Hindutva. We reached out to the Aam Aadmi Party and what I heard had me stumped. The party said *Outlook* was anti-AAP and cited a cover that we had done some years ago before I had taken over. The cover had been very harsh, describing the Aam Aadmi Party as the 'Arrogant Aadmi Party'.[1]

AAP leaders, Kejriwal included, were reportedly very upset and were reluctant to engage with *Outlook* any further. I went on an overdrive to repair the damage and put my reputation as a balanced journalist on the line. 'Give us an interview and we would do a very objective cover', we promised as both I and my political editor, Bhavna Vij-Aurora, pulled every possible string we could within the party. We insisted we would ask all the hard questions and report on every aspect, but our stories would be objective. I gave my word, and Kejriwal finally relented. We put him on the cover, with a no-holds-barred interview and extensive reportage on the upcoming elections that quoted all sides. This time, Kejriwal didn't complain.

However, two past *Outlook* covers continued to defy an easy solution and gave me constant grief. Ironically, one happened to be on the Best Chief Minister (Best Administrator to be precise), and the other was on the Worst Chief Minister of the country.

The two covers appeared at a gap of at least three years, one in 2014, and the other in 2017.[2] But both cast a long shadow that I failed to shrug off several years later. Elections in the crucial bellwether state of Uttar Pradesh were due in 2022, and we at *Outlook*, like every other media house, were on an overdrive to cover the state. What is the state of play there, can Yogi Adityanath get re-elected, will the fractious opposition manage to bury their differences, would the recent farmers' protests over the contentious farm laws turn the peasant community against the ruling BJP, will the Jats and Muslims of western UP come together to turn the tables on Adityanath – there were many questions waiting to be answered, and we naturally were interested.

We tried to speak to the various stakeholders. BSP chief Mayawati seemed a long shot as she rarely gave interviews, but Chief Minister Adityanath proved relatively easy to reach. He sat down with us for a detailed interview. Ajit Singh, a former Union minister and son of ex-prime minister Charan Singh, had passed away, passing the mantle of his Rashtriya Lok Dal (RLD) to his foreign-educated son, Jayant Chaudhary. Though a bit player in the exceptionally large state with a population equal to Germany, UK and France put together, the RLD could play a critical role in some parts of UP, particularly in western UP. Chaudhary readily agreed to meet us.

The politician who stayed elusive for much of the time we desperately tried to meet him was the one considered most important to the state's opposition camp. Akhilesh Yadav – the former chief minister and leader of the principal opposition Samajwadi Party (SP) – was clearly eyeing a return to power. The outcome of the 2022 elections depended a lot on how Akhilesh fared and whether he succeeded in tapping into the discontent that presumably existed against the state government, and how he managed to stitch together an alliance with other parties to prevent opposition votes from splitting. But Akhilesh wouldn't give us an interview, citing our 2014 cover, which described him as the 'Worst Chief Minister'.

The 2017 assembly elections in Uttar Pradesh vindicated the cover story. If not the worst, the verdict definitely showed Akhilesh Yadav as a bad chief minister – something that the *Outlook* story stated. Titled 'Dad Writ Large',[3] he was portrayed in the story as someone who was inexperienced and hemmed in by the coterie around his father, former chief minister Mulayam Singh Yadav. Appearing some three years ahead of state elections, the story was a total denunciation of whatever Akhilesh sought to project in his favour and listed out his many failings: lack of experience in politics and governance, Mulayam Singh Yadav's backseat driving, ideas and schemes started with good intent but never implemented, a casual attitude and too pliant a personality, too many power centres and senior leaders running the government like a fiefdom. Among the many things that the story stated against Akhilesh, perhaps the most damaging was the claim that he was being treated by senior party leaders and bureaucrats as a 'trainee chief minister'. Even if the story was proven right by the outcome of the 2017 state elections, Akhilesh was cut up. He carried his grudge even years later.

If the 'worst chief minister' cover caused me protracted trouble, the one on the 'best chief minister' did too. It was in 2017, a year before I took over, that *Outlook* was having its annual SpeakOut event, and decided to felicitate some personalities who had excelled in their respective fields. The event was a big success, with former president of India, Pranab Mukherjee, former vice president Hamid Ansari, and Union minister Arun Jaitley in attendance alongside a galaxy of VIPs packing the auditorium.

The highlight was the Vinod Mehta Memorial Lecture delivered by Steve Coll, the acclaimed American journalist-writer and dean of the Journalism School at Columbia University. Besides the people who shared the stage that night – to get Pranab Mukherjee and Arun Jaitley together was no mean feat – all eyes were also on the people getting the awards. Jaitley got the Best Parliamentarian award, while Wipro chairman Azim Premji got the one reserved for the Best Socially Conscious Entrepreneur category. There were several more awards that night, including Best Social Activist given to Patna-based Anand Kumar of 'Super 30' fame, and Best Academician to psychologist and social theorist Ashis Nandy.

The person who garnered the maximum attention and drew the loudest applause that night was Naveen Patnaik, Odisha's chief minister. He was feted as Best Administrator for what was said to be his illustrious work in 'bringing poverty down, ensuring growth, making Odisha a major rice producer and for his handling of the situation arising out of the cyclones that hit the coastal state.' [4]

Taciturn by nature, Patnaik generally kept to himself during the event, engaging little with anyone apart from exchanging customary greetings with the other VIPs. But the next day when he flew back to his home state, he decided to make the most of what he chose to portray as a big prestigious award. Placards and hoardings went up across Bhubaneswar and beyond, hailing him as the country's best CM. Some 10,000 frenzied members of his Biju Janata Dal (BJD) also turned up at the airport to roll out a rapturous welcome. Patnaik was taken by his ecstatic supporters in a joyous procession to his home.

The deafening din raised by Patnaik's followers that day continued to haunt me for many years. It was a remarkable coincidence that I, who have had a long association with Odisha, became *Outlook*'s editor a year after Patnaik was adjudged by the magazine as the country's best chief minister. Many forgot to take note of the timeline – that I wasn't the editor when Patnaik was feted. To many, it was I who had given the award.

Some years later, when I decided to write a book on Patnaik – the first authoritative one on the country's longest-serving chief minister, re-elected no less than five times – memories of the award continued to chase me. That a book was waiting to be written on the phenomenon of Patnaik was undisputable. No elected official at present has uninterruptedly been in power in the country for as long as Patnaik. Not even Prime Minister Modi, who was the chief minister of Gujarat from 2001 and has been the Prime Minister since 2014. First elected as chief minister in 2000, Naveen Patnaik, if he completes his current term, will equal the record of Sikkim's Pawan Kumar Chamling of being the chief minister for the longest time – twenty-four years. Patnaik, in fact, is set to surpass the record of Jyoti Basu, who was West Bengal's chief minister for a little over twenty-three years.

Not everyone, though, was convinced about my book. Even before they read what I had written, a sizeable section concluded that it must be a hagiography, since I worked for *Outlook* that had awarded the chief minister. The book turned out to be anything but that. However, questions over my alleged proximity to the chief minister never really died down.

There were other unintended consequences too. *Outlook* clearly had not thought through the pros and cons of their decision to honour Patnaik. As far as I know, there was no jury and no selection process. Having chosen Patnaik – it is said Bihar chief minister Nitish Kumar was the first choice, but he turned down the request to attend, prompting the magazine to settle for Patnaik, who readily agreed to be present – the magazine earned the displeasure of another prominent politician from Odisha, Dharmendra Pradhan.

Then Union minister for petroleum, Dharmendra saw himself as a political rival to Patnaik. As the undisputed leader of the BJP in the state, Dharmendra was eyeing the state elections scheduled for 2019 and silently nursed the desire to be the next chief minister. He spent most of his days burnishing his own image and tarnishing that of Patnaik. *Outlook*'s certificate to Patnaik as the best CM was something he never appreciated. He was clearly unhappy, and, possibly as a consequence, the advertisements that *Outlook* hoped to get from the cash-rich petroleum ministry failed to materialize. Ties between the two remained frosty for at least the next two years.

Besides the instant displeasure of a powerful Union minister, *Outlook* earned little else. Patnaik paid for several thousand extra copies of the magazine that featured him on the cover and went back. The copies mysteriously showed up for free underneath the front doors of many residents of Bhubaneswar and Cuttack in the next few days, and *Outlook* came in extremely handy to Patnaik for a publicity blitzkrieg.

My run as *Outlook*'s editor, on the contrary, fetched mixed results. Inside the office and within my own team, I found myself welcome. I settled to a comfortable routine – constantly ideating for stories and rallying up the staff for their proper execution on a weekly basis. Though I headed a weekly magazine, the job was 24/7. *Outlook* had an online portal as well, and it required hourly attention. A late starter in the online space, www.outlookindia.com had fallen behind because of neglect and lack of investment. It was time to make up for lost time.

The first time I went up to the editorial floor on the day I reported for duty, I was aghast at what I saw. Empty desks greeted me with many staffers having left the organization over a period. *Outlook* was undeniably in the midst of a financial crisis, and my first mandate was of holding the ship together. The transparent work environment that I promised minimized further attrition. Resignations still happened, but they were down to a trickle. Over the months, the editorial floor began to buzz, with fresh talent coming in, primarily drawn by the fact that *Outlook* – apart from the brand value it commanded – was a happy place, despite its financial troubles.

The outside world was rather unforgiving in contrast. As someone not well known and viewed more as a stranger, I walked into a social gathering – my first as editor – and found a group with some familiar faces in a corner. They were integral to what is known as 'Lutyens' media', and I instantly recognised them from the photographs I regularly saw. I went up and introduced myself, but in less than a minute, the group moved away, leaving me holding my glass alone.

Socially awkward – my wife tells me I talk too much when among close friends but am tongue-tied in large gatherings – acceptance was hard to come by, as illustrated by another event some months later. Vinod Mehta's family had organized a memorial lecture in his honour, and I reached the venue to find a current colleague standing in the middle of a tight circle. I went up, and the colleague introduced me to the rest, who I was then informed mostly comprised former *Outlook* staffers. So far, so good. But in a minute, the crowd dispersed, and only the colleague and I were left standing looking at each other.

Undeterred by what I saw as slights, I immersed myself in my work. There was a lot to do and that included charting a course for the magazine that would be topical as well as different. For a long time, I had felt the media suffered from bankruptcy of ideas and everyone mostly ended up doing the same stories, not told any differently. One newspaper that always impressed me was the *Indian Express*. It had limited circulation in Delhi but buzzed with a different kind of stories high on the surprise element. Its editor, Raj Kamal Jha, is someone I had always looked up to, having briefly worked with him at *India Today*.

He was in Delhi, and I in Kolkata, but we had collaborated on some amazing stories together, including one on a poor impoverished tribal couple of Odisha's Kalahandi, expecting the birth of a child as the New Year approached.[5] In 1994, *India Today* reporters accompanied by photographers had fanned across the country to document the arrival of newborns amid challenging situations that existed in the country then, from an outbreak of plague in Surat to the political upheaval in Kashmir. I travelled to Kalahandi along with photographer Prashant Panjiar to document the arrival of a baby amid back-breaking poverty. My story accompanied with a moving black-and-white photograph of the young couple taken by Prashant, formed only a part of the *India Today* cover story that appeared in January 1995 titled 'Carrying Hope,' but was the most talked about.

Moved by the plight of the couple – who incidentally had lost a child to suspected malnutrition – readers sent in money for them. The response was so overwhelming that Prashant and I were asked to go back to Kalahandi and give the couple the money that had been collected. By then, the child had been born. Having opened a bank account with the money that we carried, we named the newborn 'Sapna', and Aroon Purie wrote another editorial, thanking the readers for giving her poor parents the courage to dream. We thanked Raj Kamal. It had been his idea.

Convinced that ideas made or unmade any publication, I tried to get the best. I ideated furiously at *Outlook*. So did the senior staff. All ideas were welcome, including those from the most junior of our team members. The months passed, and the time arrived to plan our 2018 year-end issue. Important magazines such as the *Time* had made it a habit of bringing out a signature issue to mark the closure of the year gone by. They called it the 'Person of the Year' issue, profiling people who had made a mark in the past year. The most notable of them found a prized place on its cover. *Time*'s Person of the Year turned out to be a big hit. People waited for it, prompting clones even in India. Magazines such as *India Today* had something similar for their year-end issue.

Outlook in its more than twenty years of existence had made no such effort. Its year-end issue lacked character, which I decided it must have. But what could it be? I thought long and hard before concluding that we would instead have an 'Issue of the Year'. It meant we would trawl through all that had happened in the past year and zero in on the single biggest issue that impacted people's lives and the country. Everyone agreed it could be a smart template, and we sat down to decide on the most important issue for that year.

A lot of issues came up for discussion, but a decision was hard to come by. We were on the search for something that had been important and definitive but also had the quality of being somewhat different. We wanted our issue to stand out. Then Preetha Nair, a political reporter in the team, said something that had all of us jump in unison. We were meeting at a time when the country had been rocked by protests for and against the vexed issue of Sabarimala in the country's south. The Supreme Court of India had ordered some time ago that women of all ages be allowed to go on pilgrimage to the temple – something that women of menstruating age were barred from. Traditionalists believed women who menstruated were unclean and should stay away from the deity. But the court ruling opened up a Pandora's box. Women activists celebrated while others more conservative in their beliefs objected.

Soon, Kerala was swept up by an unprecedented upheaval, with even political parties such as the Congress undertaking some stunning somersaults. First, it welcomed the ruling but then opposed it on the ground of being against tradition. Does Sabarimala qualify to be the most important issue of the year? Preetha asked rather tentatively. We instantly agreed it was a great hook but soon zeroed in on menstruation as the all-important issue. Stigmatized and looked down upon, the biological phenomenon that women experienced was much misunderstood and maligned. It squarely was the main reason behind the storm over Sabarimala, and our Issue for the Year was promptly selected.

Our year-end issue, 'I Bleed for Life',[6] with a stunning painting of a woman in red on the cover, set tongues wagging. It was an extraordinarily bold cover under extremely contested circumstances, and I made no bones about it in my editorial.[7] I began by citing the case of a twelve-year-old girl, Vijaya, whose world had literally come crashing down. She lived in Thanjavur in Tamil Nadu and had been banished by her family to a shed outside her home when she menstruated for the first time in November. She stayed there for three days until a fierce storm swept the state and the shed that sheltered Vijaya collapsed on her. Vijaya died.

In as big a nation as India with more than a billion people, Vijaya's death in a far corner of the country made little difference to anyone. Most newspapers refused to give it prominence, burying it in the inside pages. Television channels besotted with scandals, celebrities and controversies also generally gave it a pass.

As always, plenty of things happened in the country in 2018. The year began with a rare press conference by four senior sitting judges of the Supreme Court that was seen to be a virtual rebellion against the then chief justice – and the open show of dissent at the top court kept the country fixated for days on end. Once fatigue set in, and the headlines moved away, the nation found other things to turn its attention to. Hima Das, the ace athlete from Assam, won laurels in the racing tracks of distant Finland while Virat Kohli continued to scorch the cricket field with sublime centuries. There were lynchings in Assam and Rajasthan that shocked us. Diamantaire Nirav Modi gave the slip after defrauding banks to our collective dismay. There was also massive outrage when several academics and activists were arrested in what seemed to be a crackdown by the government against free speech and dissent. We tracked elections held in several states closely and celebrated in unison when the Supreme Court, in a landmark judgment, decriminalized homosexuality.

But Vijaya found little space in the spotlight, and I, in my editorial, voiced deep disgust:

> Menstruation is a necessary rite of passage for women, who constitute over 48 per cent of our population. Yet, the girl was made to pay with her life for a natural biological phenomenon. India never ceases to surprise, and the stigma, prejudice and ignorance attached to menstruation is indeed baffling.
>
> Without being judgemental and abstaining from the larger debate over faith versus law, the upheaval that swept through Kerala is an astounding statement of our inability to come to terms with menstruation. Not every woman meets the fate of Vijaya. But what they are forced to endure is no less heart-breaking. Our ignorance is our collective shame, and therefore, our choice of Issue of the Year is Menstruation.

Readers overwhelmingly agreed, and the issue was a resounding success. Cracker of an issue, it was considered a collectors' item by many. Menstruation was normally not a subject that magazines around the globe thought cover-worthy. But by doing so, we clearly broke a few barriers. Also, the issue delving into various aspects of what was generally thought to be a taboo, was indeed informative. I, for one, got goosebumps reading the articles before the magazine went to press. Menstruation pads came to our home tightly wrapped in newspapers and reading what the magazine stated made me ponder about the futility of hiding what was only natural and biological.

Sara Read, the author of *Menstruation and the Female Body in Early Modern England,*[8] wrote a deeply thought-out piece, concluding that someday experiencing periods will, at last, be accepted as a natural and normal part of living in a female body. Ruma Satwik and Ambarish Satwik held forth knowledgeably on the phenomenon. 'Period pollution is a myth. What it does in biology is cleansing a monthly exorcism of pathogens', they pointed out.

Noted lawyer, Indira Jaising, shed light on the physical taboo at Sabarimala and the verbal one playing out in the country's courts, while others, from Arshia Dhar and Lachmi Deb Roy, focused on the folk arts and menstruation and the importance of period leave.

While we wallowed in positive feedback, there was no time to waste. Months later, India would hold its general elections, and we worked overtime to make our mark again. We wanted to be different in our coverage of the 2019 polls and did our best without sacrificing any of the sight, sound and colour that accompanied elections. While most of the media focused on quotes – he said and she said types – and customary analysis of which way the vote may go, we charted an unusual course.

We rolled out our coverage by devoting a cover on India's Chanakyas – decoding the men and women who made up the durbars of the most famous leaders, providing them inputs and strategic counsel on political manoeuvres. We all know a lot about the Patnaiks and Biswa Sarmas but little about their backroom boys. Our cover focused on them – who they were and what they did. From V.K. Pandian, the IAS officer and the Odisha chief minister's trusted aide, considered the second most influential person in the state, to Ramchandra Prasad Singh, the man quietly shaping Bihar chief minister Nitish Kumar's political destiny.[9]

We strived to think out of the box, and the issues in the run-up to the elections bore the stamp of innovative ideas. We looked at elections through the prism of hotspots – from Kashmir to Ayodhya and Mandsaur to understand how issues such as nationalism, Ram Mandir and farmers' distress were likely to play out. Amid the high-octane campaign dominated by prominent leaders, in one of our subsequent issues, we trained our eyes on the foot-soldiers –

ordinary party workers who form the backbone of political parties and are on the frontlines of the election battle, often at the cost of their lives or limbs.[10]

There was also a cover devoted to the phenomenon of slogans, starting with their origin and growing acceptance as a potent political weapon and how exactly they impacted polls. 'If politics is in our blood, the slogan is the pulse. Its rhythms aren't partisan; they create a community of words', wrote our managing editor Sunil Menon, as we looked at how slogans – from *Samose Mein Aloo, Bihar Mein Lalu* to *Phir Ek Baar Modi Sarkar* – have come to define our political journey. We rightly titled the cover 'Slogans Zindabad'.[11]

The results were satisfying. At a time when print media circulations were supposedly going down everywhere – particularly of magazines – *Outlook*'s print run showed signs of improvement. Our different kind of content began to be noticed and, by the end of the first year, our circulation had grown by some 10 per cent. But we were not out of the woods yet, and the going was far from smooth. Besides being low, salaries that were paid erratically remained a constant source of concern. When I joined, salaries would be paid within the said month, but normally in the second or third week. The delays gradually got longer and by the time the pandemic hit in 2020, things got infinitely worse.

Arrears piled up – by as much as five months – and my troubles mounted. I began to dread every new month with staff sending SOS for unpaid salaries. Emails started flooding my inbox and desperation grew. People had rents to pay, which many were unable to. At least a few got thrown out by landlords and morale hit a low. Resignations – particularly from the younger lot on the digital desk – became regular. The entire team changed twice over. Holding the fort in the face of extreme adversity became a big challenge.

Fortunately, though, the quality of *Outlook*'s journalism survived the testing times. We still managed to do some stellar work, staying ahead of the curve while chronicling the Covid19-induced crisis that had befallen the country. Beginning with 'Covid Warriors',[12] we covered the catastrophe in detail – from the potential food crisis to the crumbling state of mental health of a population suddenly held hostage by a virus. Much before anyone else, we ran a cover story on nurses – those who risked their lives to save ours – wondering aloud whether we were grateful enough to them.

In another issue, we looked at life and death, profiling families who were grieving the death of a loved one or celebrating the arrival of a newborn under the harsh lockdown necessitated by the pandemic. In rolling out new covers, we resorted to some fun as well and coined a new word: 'Covided'.[13] One of our issues looked at things that the onset of the pandemic had undone, or rather got Covided: from IPL to Shaheen Bagh protests and the price of mangoes that crashed with people forced indoors.

We believed we scored some talking points with our stand-out covers. But money matters – or the inability to pay the staff and contributors on time – got talked about as prominently. As the public face of the magazine, I got used to being targeted on social media – whatever be the reason. Every now and then, whenever subscribers found that they were not getting *Outlook* copies despite paying the subscription, they were prompt to tweet tagging me that they were being cheated. Some indeed used cuss words and cursed.

For that matter, I also regularly got complaints from former *Outlook* interns working with other departments – marketing and circulation – that they had not been paid the dues they had been promised. I had nothing to do with them, yet I regularly got the stick. For example, one individual wrote to me, saying she had worked as a sales and marketing intern from January to March and, despite her repeated reminders, she had still not been paid. It was already August. Minus a resolution, many chose to air their grievances publicly.

Far more serious was the situation with the staff. Already struggling to clear salaries on time, the pandemic and the accompanying lockdown worsened *Outlook*'s financial state. Steep salary cuts were announced across the board – for me, it was 50 per cent. But what hurt the most was that it came into effect retrospectively. *Outlook*'s CEO in an email on 30 May 2020 underlined the gravity of the financial stress and announced the cuts from April. So, basically, staff who had worked for April and May under the impression they would get the money that their contracts stipulated were now being told they would get a far less amount.

It triggered immediate consternation. One young colleague put his foot down and insisted the cuts could not be retrospective. April salaries had been delayed, and he argued in an email that 'there's no way an employee can be made to accept pay cuts retrospectively when it was the company's fault not to pay them on time'. His argument was sound but failed to cut ice. First, he tried to go on protest leave. When that was not allowed, he quit, asking that all his dues be cleared in full. The management dragged its feet, saying the final payment would be with the cuts. The colleague threatened to go to court, and the matter was settled. But the bad blood left us all scarred.

More such disagreements arose within the office. It was the time for frenetic cost-cutting to keep the organization afloat, and even lowly-paid office peons lost their jobs. One young reporter with a flair for writing lost his cool. Hired by me, he was the team's blue-eyed boy. But as salaries got progressively reduced and delayed, he wrote me an anguished mail. 'Dear Editor, I hold you in great regard and for the same reason, I had held myself from writing this mail for over a month. But the situation has become unbearable, and I can't keep this with me any further. We haven't got our salaries for four months now. Four months! How are we to manage our expenses? My rent is due in two days. How am I going to pay? Just how? Things have reached a tipping point.'

I shared his angst but could do little. He went on to write in the same email: 'It goes without saying that I have had the deepest respect for your editorship. And *Outlook* beyond a shadow of doubts, has been an excellent, enriching and enjoyable workplace. But the management's handling of the crisis has been abominable. How can we go on like this? Keep the news machine running while totally shutting out the acute concerns of the employees?'

His words stung, but he was not finished yet. 'I believe you are a very fair man. Please place yourself in place of the employee and think what they are going through. It just can't go on like this … Please, think of the employees', he added. Extremely impressionable, he seemed deeply disturbed, particularly by the fact that *Outlook* was letting go of even office peons with meagre salaries.

As the editor of an organization that stood on an extremely shaky financial edifice, I tried to reason with him:

> The issues you raise are mostly valid and have been constantly in my mind. They [di]stress me at times since no immediate solution is in sight. Faced with what we are, I can only think of two options: either I throw up my hand in surrender and walk away, or we stick around and go through this in the hope that all this will finally be sorted. After careful consideration, I have chosen the second. That we are in a sticky situation is undeniable. But I have every reason to believe that the management is doing their best to regularize salaries, though they themselves might have been hit hard by the market downturn … I still believe we can pull through this and pursue our kind of quality journalism.

My words failed to satisfy him, and he quit. I decided to carry on, even if it meant some personal sacrifices.

Cost-cutting being the primary objective, *Outlook*'s management suggested I take over as editor of *Outlook Money* and *Outlook* Hindi. I agreed at no extra cost. In fact, my original salary, by then, had already been halved. With me in charge of two additional magazines, it allowed us to abolish some positions and save some money. I was convinced that to protect the jobs of 70 per cent of the staff; we would have to sacrifice some 30 per cent – however unfair and cruel it might be for those on the chopping block.

The suffering continued well into 2021 when the organization suggested that I take over as the group editor-in-chief. It meant the responsibilities of two more magazines – *Outlook Traveller* and *Outlook Business*. I again agreed at no extra cost. I was now the editor of five magazines, but with just 50 per cent of the salary that I was to originally get as the editor of only *Outlook* magazine.

I still stayed the course. Of course, there were some cursory conversations with the management about a possible hike, but I cut it short. I told them that I wouldn't be able to come to terms with my own conscience on securing a raise when my team was still reeling from deep salary cuts. As chief editor, I also gave my consent to some fresh hiring at costs higher than my own salary. I slept well in the following nights, secure in the belief that my personal sacrifices would be acknowledged and that I could get myself a raise later when we finally tided over the crisis. Overhearing some of my conversations, my wife said I was being plain stupid. I didn't care to listen to her then. But now, in hindsight, I believe she was right. I was wrong.

Journalism has given me a life-long kick, and I got it in plenty while at the helm of *Outlook*. We never ran out of ideas, and our covers continued to make waves, at least from time to time. Hathras happened, shocking India. The brutality of what a poor Dalit girl in a village in Uttar Pradesh was forced to endure was stomach-churning. First, she was raped and assaulted. When she died, the police spirited her body away and cremated her in the dead of night. Stripped of dignity in life, she was given an undignified funeral.

For *Outlook*, a lot depended on Yogi Adityanath, the state chief minister. His government was one of our biggest advertisers – spending as much as Rs 70 lakh per month. The financial implications surely weighed on our minds, but we did not baulk while covering the story. As the editor in such trying times, I was to tread a fine line – pursue honest journalism without upsetting the financial applecart. And we did that in an issue soon after the incident at Hathras had shocked us.

'She, the Dalit', screamed *Outlook*'s cover as we focused on Hathras and beyond. Yes, we didn't make Adityanath the target.

But at the same time, we didn't leave much unsaid. In my editorial that set the tone for the rest of the issue, I wrote:

> What happened in Hathras was brutality of unimaginable magnitude. Insensitive and arrogant officials turned it into an even bigger nightmare for the victim's family and friends … Despite being dulled into silent acceptance of rampant sexual crimes, including no less than the 87 rapes reported in the country a day, Hathras crossed the collective threshold of what we could digest.
>
> An insensitive state government manned by arrogant babus heaped more indignities on the dead girl … amid the injustices that abound, what happened to the Hathras girl is shocking, but not entirely surprising. While we all run the risk of running afoul of our rulers at some point of time, it is the poorest and those at the lowest rung of the perceived social order who are the most vulnerable. In this issue, we turn our gaze on those who have been traditionally weak and historically ignored: Dalit women. Hope they get a voice.[14]

I was hoping my luck would hold as well. Though never in the face, *Outlook* continued to say what needed to be said, be it during the protests at Shaheen Bagh, or the tumult in Kashmir. We never shied away from taking a stand – on the increasing number of detentions of activists and academics across the country to the growing inertia that seemed to afflict the top judiciary which many felt had all but abdicated its responsibility.

Outlook's management remained non-interfering – at least during the first three years of my editorship – and I had little reason to complain editorially. Of course, I had my share of detractors who never tired of saying that I was doing a very poor job. But there was also a sizeable section that was full of praise. One such was Manoj Kumar Jha, the articulate member of parliament, made more famous by his stirring speech criticizing the government for its alleged failures in the handling of the Covid second surge.[15]

In my first interaction with him at his residence in Delhi, Jha was generous with his compliments. 'You have taken *Outlook* to a different level', he said, even going to the extent of saying I was doing better than our legendary founding editor Vinod Mehta. 'The circumstances now are far more difficult than what he faced', Jha said. I was both elated and embarrassed. But little did I realize then that the circumstances would turn infinitely worse for me in a short while. I was clearly on thin ice, which caved in without much notice. It caught me totally by surprise.

6

THE IMMORALITY OF MORAL CLARITY

It was the moment that Rana Ayyub spoke that the loudest cheers swept through the spacious and packed hall. The occasion was the much-awaited Jaipur Literary Festival of 2020, and the discussion taking place in the evening featuring Ayyub and some veterans of the industry was on the state of Indian media. Panel discussions with high-profile guests are a highlight of the festival, and I happened to be in Jaipur as an invited panellist.

My session on almost a similar subject was in the morning, and I had shared the podium with Faye D'Souza, the noted TV anchor, and Sonia Singh of NDTV. Our discussion went well. My co-panellists were known names, and the audience agreed when they said that the media in India was not in good health. They even agreed when I said that newsrooms in the country had been politicized and polarized. We drew intermittent applause.

It was nothing in comparison to the reaction to Ayyub later in the day. For one, Ayyub is a well-known journalist with a massive following on social media such as Twitter, where she has more than one million followers. Also, her work as an exceptionally brave journalist is widely talked about. But what has made her controversial is her book, *The Gujarat Files*[1], documenting what she alleged was the complicity of top Gujarat officials in the communal riots that rocked the state post-Godhra. She claimed to have gone undercover and recorded officials and politicians openly boasting about their roles in abetting the 2002 riots and allowing the perpetrators to sidestep the long arm of the law.[2]

The book was a massive hit. It sold in lakhs and was translated into several languages, giving Ayyub the reputation of being one of the feistiest journalists of our times. Not everyone agrees with her journalism, though. She seems to hate Prime Minister Modi and Home Minister Amit Shah almost viscerally. She is extremely critical of the ruling BJP – both in Gujarat and at the Centre – and never has anything good to say about them. Given her stated positions, Ayyub is regarded as anti-Modi. What she writes and what she says almost invariably evoke divisive responses. Not many publications in India are willing to publish her. But she writes regularly for papers abroad, including the *Washington Post*, and her articles raise the hackles of hardcore BJP supporters who see her as an 'anti-national'. But then there is also a vociferous section that idolizes her as a fearless journalist taking on the establishment at huge personal risk.

At Jaipur, Ayyub lived up to her reputation as a vocal critic of PM Modi. She was acerbic in her denunciation of how things were in the country and in her critique of the media – TV and print included – which she said had all but abdicated its responsibility in holding the mirror to those in power. She struck an immediate chord with the audience, which crowded the auditorium. That the media had become subservient and peddled narratives that suited those in power was a widely held belief and every word spoken by Ayyub was lapped up. Ayyub, too, did not seem to be in a hurry to let up on the verbal fusillade that she had launched. Perhaps sensing the mood of the audience, she played to the gallery and claimed all good journalists in the country had either been sacked or had resigned. 'There is no good journalist with a job in the country', she said amid even louder cheers.

Sitting in the crowd, I heard her with growing mortification. I agreed to a large extent with what she said but couldn't agree fully. I hadn't been sacked yet by *Outlook* – it happened more than a year later – I still had a job. Also, if not good, I considered myself to be an honest journalist who did his job diligently. Besides, I had no reason to believe that the profession was entirely devoid of good journalists, though I agreed that their numbers were dwindling alarmingly.

Whatever be the dismal state of the media, I still had reason to be proud of the work at least some of the journalists did. Among others, Somesh Jha's name came instantly to my mind. I didn't know Jha, but his reporting on the state of the economy and rising unemployment for the *Business Standard* newspaper had been eye-openers. They knocked the bottom off government claims, and they certainly qualified to be considered great journalism.[3] Jha had well and truly exposed the government.[4]

I returned from Jaipur, pondering over the panel featuring Ayyub. I felt deeply disturbed. Both Ayyub and the response of the delirious audience to whatever she said convinced me that we as a country were more divided and polarized than I had ever imagined. The middle-ground – moderation if I may say so – was wholly missing, and we now were clearly either for or against in our personal beliefs. I didn't disagree with Ayyub. But I couldn't agree with her entirely.

The trenchant position that she articulated that day was proof that the media, too, was totally polarized. If a section blindly supported the government, the other hated it. The stark divide militated against the basic values that an old-fashioned journalist like me had grown up with and cherished: that we should be balanced and objective, giving both sides of a story. We should have the grace to accept and acknowledge if someone – no matter how opposed we are to that person – does something good. We ought to also have the courage to stand up and criticize that person if he or she does something wrong.

I believed from the bottom of my heart that we needed to be fair and balanced – something that seemed to be nowhere in sight at what was discussed at the panel. Returning to Delhi, I shared my disappointment and worries with other *Outlook* editors. We decided to do a cover on the divided media – the Great Media Divide – for the next week. We all agreed that it was a legitimate story to do. And why not? The media constantly scrutinizes others – politicians and everyone else. It was time to turn our gaze on ourselves – the media.

Just when we got ready to put out the media cover, a huge embarrassment blew up in our faces. A fortnight earlier, we had done a cover on 'The Muslims'[5] – marking the ongoing CAA agitation and the subsequent churning within the community – and the package included a column by a contributor on one of the iconic Muslims of the country – former president A.P.J. Abdul Kalam. That he was a role model – irrespective of caste, creed, and religion – was never in doubt, but the columnist had some other ideas and sneaked in, rather unnecessarily, a few disparaging remarks against the late president.

Our editorial desk should have caught them, but one blunder led to another. The editor who had commissioned the column inexplicably forgot about it till very late, when the magazine was only hours away from going to press. The desk frantically called him, and he hurriedly sent it in. With the deadline very close, the desk dropped its guard. They presumed the editor had already vetted the column, and let it pass – with the disparaging remarks – without taking a closer look. The magazine got printed, and we had a huge problem on our hands.

I lost my cool, discovering it the next day when the printed magazine landed on my desk. I shouted and screamed, but the damage was done. Knowing that the uncharitable remarks would be noticed, I initiated corrective measures. The whole magazine gets uploaded online, but this time, I ordered that the problematic column be held back. Then I wrote an apology to be published the following week and sent it to the production desk. Having done whatever we could, we waited. It was not long before the uproar over the column began. I was massively trolled on social media. My defence that it was a genuine mistake and not intentional – that it had slipped through our editorial gatekeeping – cut little ice. Abusive posts flooded in, with some even suggesting that I quit journalism and start a 'pakoda' shop instead. Some newspapers picked up the story, and *Outlook* got a bad name. Apart from suffering in silence, we could only curse its timing.

Reeling from the own-goal, I, in my editorial[6] that set the context for the divided media cover, pleaded for a fair hearing. '*Aap Chronology Samajhiye*', I sought to explain, laying out the sequence of events that led to the big mistake on our part. I tried to be as contrite as possible, hoping the readers would understand and forgive. Acknowledging the timing of the mistake could not have been more inopportune, I admitted our own credibility had ironically taken a hit while we were pontificating on the media. I even accepted the opprobrium that came our way, saying we deserved every bit of it.

Taking the criticism in stride, I reiterated that credibility remained at the core of our existence and the media, *Outlook* included, must do everything within its means to repair and reclaim it. News was supposed to be sacrosanct. But over time, it has degenerated into a kind of nuisance. It has become partisan too. Much of our information depends on which channel or newspaper we are watching/reading. A prime example of the conflicting coverage was the violence at Delhi's JNU. While some media outlets rightly viewed the students who were beaten up as victims, there were others who denounced them as no less than criminals.

Outlook's media cover voiced what bothered many of us and my editorial echoed that. 'True, we all have opinions, and we need to take an editorial stand on things that we value. But that should not give us the liberty to twist news in the manner much of the mainstream media is presenting these days. In these polarized times, what is most alarming is the argument that the concept of media neutrality is outdated. According to its votaries, objectivity is passe and it is alright for the media to present news in a manner that buttresses its point of view. That's outrageous ...,' I wrote, while the cover image sought to capture what I talked about.

On one side were the images of journalists Siddharth Varadarajan, Faye D'Souza and Magsaysay award winner Ravish Kumar. On the other side were the TV anchors Arnab Goswami, Navika Kumar and Sudhir Chaudhary. Comparing Ravish with Sudhir, or Faye with Navika, were as good as trying to draw parallels between chalk and cheese. But the two sides, we felt, were representative of two strands of journalism and showcased the great divide that had engulfed the Indian media.

Never a fan of those firmly on the side of the government, *Outlook* edited by me obviously didn't have anything good to say about those now infamously known as 'Godi Media'.[7] The term that has now found wide acceptance is a derisive description of those who apparently sit comfortably on the government's lap and unabashedly do its bidding. They faithfully parrot the government line, unfailingly defend ministers, bureaucrats and their policies, doggedly target those in the opposition and shamelessly try to spin and deflate any criticism of the government. What they practise certainly goes against the basic grain of the media's existence. The very default setting of a free and responsible media is expectedly anti-establishment, as it is required to hold the mirror to those in power. Unquestioning loyalty towards the establishment is no journalism, and *Outlook* abhorred it – despite the redlines set by the promoters on the very first day I joined.

Though not as strident as Varadarajan or Ayyub, *Outlook* consistently took a stand against the government – be it Shaheen Bagh or JNU and the dismal state of human rights in the country. That the Varadarajans and Ayyubs are phenomenally brave has never been in any doubt. They command awe and respect. But our media cover made it clear that we didn't wholly agree with their brand of journalism. If you visit The Wire, edited by Varadarajan or choose to read Ayyub, you know what you will get. They would be bitterly critical of Modi, the government and the BJP, with little or no representation of opinion from that side. In our view, that was problematic.

For us, journalism needed to give both sides. Give space to every shade of opinion – as long as it is not abusive or a call to violence. Allow debate and discussion that help readers to be better informed and draw their own conclusions. And having represented all shades of views, of course, editors reserve their right to give their own opinion as I frequently did in my editorials. We believed that was the right thing to do, even at the cost of being pilloried by one of the most junior staff members of the *Outlook* team on our own platform.

It was the first anniversary of the violence in Delhi's JNU, which saw armed goons descending on the campus and attacking students while the police strangely stood mute witness outside.[8] We decided to mark the occasion and invited a cross-section of stakeholders to write. Aishe Ghosh, president of the JNU Students' Union and one of the victims of the attack, wrote. So did Abhishek Mishra, a BJP youth leader. Aishe wrote what we overwhelmingly agreed with, that JNU – despite being a centre of excellence – was under attack for its liberal values.[9] Mishra, on the contrary, took a different line of argument, insisting that JNU must get rid of 'anti-national forces'. He then sought to augment his argument by repeating unsubstantiated allegations against Aishe and her fellow students who were assaulted. According to him, they were the perpetrators and not the victims that day.[10]

Though not convinced about what Mishra contended, we carried his article and Aishe's. Both were fine with me. They were opinions, after all – one convincing and the other not. But objections came from Salik Ahmad, our young reporter. At an editorial meeting that we had days after the two articles were carried online, he expressed his strong disagreement with my decision to allow Mishra's piece to be published. 'Editor, you are wrong', he said.

An internal debate followed, and I told him to write down his resentment. 'Feel free to go hammer and tongs against me. We will publish what you feel', I told him, convinced about the virtue of both-sides journalism. Always a fine writer, what Salik wrote was a wholesome denunciation of my editorial call. He termed Mishra's argument a lie and said: 'When I flagged the fallacy, you said it's so and so's opinion. A lie is not an opinion. Plus, an argument cannot be mounted on lies and unsubstantiated allegations, which the piece is riddled with. We cannot wash our hands of it by saying that it's another person's opinion. By publishing it, we gave it legitimacy. We normalized it. Amplified it.'[11]

Salik's piece horrified many in the team. It was unusual for a reporter to take on his own editor on the very platform that they worked for. But honestly, his critique did not bother me a bit. Perhaps, old school and possibly old fashioned, my belief that every story has two sides – however contradictory – has always run deep and been firm. Though it was fashionable of late for journalists to talk about the need for moral clarity – meaning they must take a stand for and against and cancel the opposite view – I didn't subscribe to it.

I wasn't even swayed by their argument that the situation in the country was black and white, so much so that it was akin to when it rained: you really didn't need to put your hand out to check if it was raining and take the counterview that it was not raining. If it was raining, it was raining, proponents of moral clarity argue. But even this argument didn't sound necessarily true for me. Living in Delhi, notorious for raining in some parts and not raining in others, you could not be sure it was raining in Connaught Place when it was in Chittaranjan Park. You still had to put your hands out and verify.

Firm in my belief, I allowed Salik's piece to go online, and soon it went viral. His argument provided a lot of food for thought, and even the *Washington Post* picked it up in its daily newsletter. More than anything else, the fact that a reporter had taken his editor to the cleaners set tongues wagging. I gloated in my public embarrassment. In fact, it was further proof of my own convictions. And I happily wrote in my own counter,[12] that appeared two days later, that I was more elated than embarrassed. 'A colleague has shown spine and spoken up and that is something we must acknowledge and cherish. None of us are infallible and not all decisions of ours are beyond reproach. And since we are all likely to come to wrong conclusions at certain times, scrutiny of what we do is always to be welcomed. To that extent, Salik was absolutely right, and I sincerely wish more power to him.'

However, I stood by my belief in both-sides journalism and held forth on the virtues of listening to all sides. I wrote:

> The polity is divided and so are we. As positions become rigid, it has become somewhat fashionable to take a strident stand even if it means shutting down the voice of the other side completely. A stand we must take. For, as the famous American journalist of Watergate fame Carl Bernstein reminded us

> during a recent visit, it should necessarily be on the side of the best obtainable version of the truth. And how do you arrive at the best obtainable version of the truth? Of course, by not precluding any side and listening to all versions.

For that matter, Salik's contrarian piece wouldn't have found a place on our platform but for my unflinching belief in both-sides journalism. *Outlook* practised precisely that during my editorship, and the issue with the divided media on the cover was no different. We didn't hide our dislike for the sycophantic media. But we didn't shut them up either. We heard them by giving space to what they said, and for that, we commissioned R. Jagannathan – known to be an editor with right-wing sympathies – to write. As expected, Jagannathan was critical of the Lutyen's Media that *Outlook* was supposedly part of. He held our portrayal of the anti-CAA agitation as secular as hypocritical and claimed the joke was now on the mainstream media, 'which is still claiming neutrality when its sympathies are obvious to everyone and the dog at the lamp-post'.[13]

Though not entirely convincing, Jagannathan made a strong case justifying the media divide in India:

> There is a good reason why this polarization has come out in the open now rather than earlier. Until about a decade ago, only one side controlled the media … this ecosystem's stranglehold in both media and academia ensured that there was only one dominant narrative about India. With digital taking centre stage over the past decade, new voices sprang up to question the mainstream narrative. Today, even if you are an editor with pro-Congress views, you cannot stop other journalists in your own organization from blogging differently. The tyranny of

> controlling the narrative from the top of the editorial hierarchy is dying, if not dead. Today's media polarization is a direct result of the smashing of the monopoly on narrative-setting by Lutyen's Delhi, which has not taken kindly to being challenged repeatedly by upstart journalists from the right.

The editors at *Outlook* were wholly against narrative-setting by cancelling out contrarian views. We disagreed with Jagannathan on many scores but had no qualms running his piece. We didn't even agree how the 'upstart journalists from the right' that Jagannathan eulogized pursued their craft by often falling back on news that was fake. Yet, what Jagannathan said had to be heard since cancelling contrarian opinion had intrinsic shortcomings and would inevitably lead to unwelcome suppression. I don't agree with a view, and I don't publish it. The others don't agree with me, and they shut me out. With both righteously cancelling each other, what you have resultantly is nothing but unmitigated censorship.

Most importantly, who decides whose views are correct? *Outlook* wasn't right when ahead of the 2014 general elections, it pompously proclaimed on its cover in September 2013 that Narendra Modi wouldn't become the Prime Minister. 'No, He Can't'[14] – the cover headline said even though a large majority of Indians had already made up their minds to vote for Modi and his BJP. That the ruling Congress-led UPA, singed by successive scandals, was hugely unpopular and that Modi was at the peak of his popularity was never in doubt. But perhaps some editors at *Outlook* then chose to rely on their personal beliefs more than popular perceptions. None of them was any less honest than me. They could also take the plea that in deciding on such a cover, they were only trying to be truthful to what they genuinely believed was moral clarity. Modi's victory in the elections, however, showed up the inadequacies of such clarity. None of us was error-proof though we may be under the illusion of possessing moral clarity.

The embarrassing cover had lessons for me: it told me to be more circumspect when it came to making editorial calls. I also learnt not to get too carried away. We did and said things that seemed right but never indulged in careless bravado. It didn't make sense for an organization that employed hundreds of people. Imperilling livelihoods for the cheap thrill of hyperbole defied logic.

My focus was always on honest journalism without appearing to be unnecessarily feisty or disproportionately daring. That's why *Outlook* wasn't exactly like *Caravan*, a magazine which I greatly valued and subscribed to. But for its irregular supply – they rarely arrived though I was an annual subscriber – *Caravan*'s strident criticism of the government wasn't something *Outlook* could afford. Though it may come across as politically incorrect, caution for the most part of my editorship remained the guiding principle as I strived to do everything within my means to facilitate that *Outlook* earned revenue, paid salaries to staff and enabled us to pursue our craft.

This meant aligning oneself with the management when it made efforts to earn revenue. The market was bad, and money was in short supply. Magazine sales and subscriptions hardly covered the costs, and we were reliant on advertisements, mostly from governments, for our survival. This explains why I had to visit politicians in office from time to time, including Uttar Pradesh Chief Minister Adityanath. With an eye on upcoming elections, the Uttar Pradesh government was on a publicity overdrive. It was advertising big time, and *Outlook* too pitched for its share.

Face to face with Adityanath, I played my part, promising to cover the state and the chief minister as extensively as possible. I gave a caveat, though: 'We will not do anything unethical'. He nodded in silent agreement, and his government opened its purse strings for *Outlook*, too, giving as much as Rs 70 lakh a month in advertisements to the various magazines of the group. The extra revenue was a much-needed reprieve for the staff that had been hit hard by salary cuts and delays. Salaries, though reduced, reverted to a thirty-day cycle, even as we put Yogi Adityanath on the cover several times – in *Outlook* English,[15] and in *Outlook* Hindi.

We were certainly not singing paeans to Adityanath. We raised pertinent points and challenged him on various issues – from Hathras to the bodies that floated on the Ganga during the second surge of Covid. Even critics of the Uttar Pradesh government found adequate space. For that matter, the last idea for an *Outlook* cover that I pitched as the magazine's editor was to focus on Adityanath's controversial 'Abba Jaan' comment. With assembly elections months away, the chief minister of India's largest state was clearly trying to polarize the electorate by employing communal rhetoric. One such example was his claim that food rations the poor are entitled to were mostly cornered during earlier regimes by those belonging to a minority community. '*Ration sabko mil raha hai?…tab toh abbajaan kehne wale rashan hazam kar jaate the*' (Is everybody getting their share of food rations? … Then [before 2017], those who called their father abbajaan would monopolize it), he said.[16]

But the suggested cover could not get done. I did not survive as the editor much longer, causing grief and disappointment. By then, however, dejection had become a part of life. We were as dejected when our 'Great Media Divide' cover[17] failed to make any difference to the manner the media conducted itself. No lessons were learnt, and some months later, the media outraged us even more than before.

Starting his nightly TV show, one particularly partisan but popular anchor served loud notice that he didn't agree at all with *Outlook*'s journalism. 'What a fall for a magazine once edited by Vinod Mehta', he ranted, venting his displeasure at our recent cover on the media trial that had the country transfixed in the wake of the death of Bollywood star Sushant Singh Rajput in June 2020. It happened at a time when India was firmly in the grip of the Covid pandemic, but the media trial portraying the actor's girlfriend, Rhea Chakraborty, as being primarily responsible for his untimely death was what kept the nation hooked.

Beginning 14 June, the day when the actor's lifeless body was found hanging at his Mumbai apartment,[18] large sections of the Indian media started having a field day, freely speculating about the actor's death. They first talked about nepotism that dominated India's top entertainment industry and gossiped about what could have pushed the immensely talented Rajput to his death. For days on end, the talk centred around how the actor struggled to find work and how entrenched interests in Bollywood deprived him of what was due to him. Then suddenly, the media turned its gaze on Rhea – turning her life upside down.

Rhea was easy prey. Young, outgoing and ambitious, she was an aspiring actress yet to find her feet in the madly competitive world of Hindi films. She worked, partied and dressed in a manner that didn't conform to patriarchal mindsets, and when the media made her out to be the villain, there were ready takers. As frenzied media scrums stalked her relentlessly, she found herself helplessly at the receiving end of baseless allegations. The allegations were ridiculous, to say the least, but media houses competed against each other to come up with more bizarre ones. People seemed to have an insatiable appetite for unsubstantiated accusations and lapped them up.

Television Rating Points (TRPs) of television channels soared as Rhea became headline news and rapidly grew into a national obsession. From feeding off Rajput's wealth to plying him with drugs, Rhea stood accused of many misdeeds.[19] She attempted to give an interview and set the record straight. But few listened, and she was shortly arrested by the Narcotics Control Bureau (NCB) for procuring a minuscule quantity of marijuana.[20] Some three crore people of India are known to use marijuana[21] – something that is permitted in many countries but banned in India. But Rhea was singled out, and several television channels ran campaigns to get her arrested. When she was – she spent nearly a month in jail – it was hailed as a victory of good over evil.

For us at *Outlook*, though, the unmitigated media circus was the death of journalism. We decided to speak out against the travesty of justice, even if it meant going against the overwhelming public mood which saw Rhea vilified mercilessly. Among everything else, she was on the cover of Bhojpuri albums that characterized her as a 'loose woman'.[22] Undeterred, we chose to run a cover that had an image of Rhea holding a slate that the police often make suspects hold with their names and contact details. But the slate that she held on *Outlook*'s cover[23] made a very powerful statement. 'Accused, Tried, Convicted,' it proclaimed, underlining the fact that every accused is considered innocent unless proven guilty by the court of law.

The inside pages of the issue were as powerful. In summing up the madness surrounding the show trial that had India fixated, reporter Prashant Srivastava was caustic in his criticism of journalists: '… the media appears to be in a tearing hurry to take the case to its conclusion, logical or not, without bothering to wait for the findings of law enforcement agencies or, for that matter, for the judicial process. Today, the average TV journalist subsumes all those roles in an all-in-one justice system; the media is by itself investigator, prosecutor, jury, judge … and executioner.'[24]

Rhea Chakraborty's media trial was certainly not the first to have rocked the country. There were many before, including when Congress MP Shashi Tharoor found himself in the midst of one following the death of his wife, Sunanda Pushkar.[25] Chasing TRPs, television reporters had chased and hounded Tharoor, too, as relentlessly as they pursued Rhea, with one television anchor even going to the extent of claiming that the politician had been surrounded by his crew and that he would not be allowed to escape.[26] Tharoor, however, escaped finally, with a court in Delhi absolving him of any role in his wife's death.[27] Ironically, Republic TV, the channel that made the most noise over Tharoor's alleged complicity, blacked out the news of his exoneration. It pretended it was business as usual and gave the Tharoor story a quiet burial.

Rhea's media trial has also followed a somewhat similar trajectory. All fire and brimstone in the initial months, the offending channels went strangely quiet at the first anniversary of Rajput's death. In the year gone by, investigative agencies failed to make any headway and couldn't come up with evidence of Rhea's involvement in his death. In the absence of proof after a year of probing, the channels pretended nothing was amiss. Their immediate purpose of boosting viewership achieved; they forgot to follow up on the story that they had promised to pursue till the very end.

Outlook's cover stood vindicated a year on. But there was actually little reason to pat ourselves on the back. No lessons have been learnt and the Indian media very much remains a loose cannon, ready to launch a witch-hunt at the slightest opportunity. The media continues to struggle for revenue and TRPs to lure advertisers remain as strong an allurement as ever. What if journalism is turned upside down and basic principles of justice given short shrift in the process? It does not augur well for the future, but then few tears will be shed for the rapid decline in media's standards.

The downhill journey began a long time ago with old-timers pointing out that many journalists and the organizations they worked for were found to be crawling before politicians in power even during the Emergency of the mid-1970s. We now cower, and the trend is unlikely to be halted anytime soon. Survival is the key for most media organizations, and no one is seemingly perturbed over falling standards. Good journalism, too, isn't the primary objective, with the company's balance sheets increasingly taking priority. This alone perhaps explains why a top media house in Delhi chose to carpet bomb interior regions with 'sources'. Earlier, the group in question appointed stringers – reporters on a monthly retainership – to report from blocks and districts of any state. Later, those retainers were redesignated simply as sources. They worked without the promise of payments but were required to file reports and also procure advertisements against a certain percentage as commission from small builders and contractors of the region they operated in. I encountered them on a trip to a small town of Uttar Pradesh, with at least three sources showing up at my door. Operating within a demarcated geographical space, they competed with each other more to get advertisements than news. That remained their only shot at sustenance.

It illustrated how badly Indian media's structure is skewed. The industry falls essentially in the unorganized sector, with editors and full-time journalists on the rolls of media houses accounting for only a minuscule section of working journalists. The influence and attention that they wield – particularly those in Delhi and state capitals – are abnormally disproportionate to their numbers. Delhi journalists, for example, hog the limelight for their proximity to TV studios, while the bulk of the actual work of journalism is left to the network of freelancers and stringers spread across rural India.

Though not necessarily dismissed by all as sources, they do not fare much better. Minus reasonable pay and protection that a full-time job as defined by the Working Journalist Act, originally adopted in 1955, provide, they are up against heavy odds. Many are enticed into taking shortcuts and resorting to blackmail. Those who stand firm on their principles regularly pay a heavy price. Journalists who get killed or assaulted in a country that ranks very low in the global Press Freedom Index are mostly them.[28] But for the perfunctory condemnations from various press clubs or the occasional candle-lit vigils held in their honour, little succour is in sight for them.

That the media's future looks bleak was evident from my perch as *Outlook*'s editor. Of course, there is some phenomenal work happening, including by some in an otherwise vitiated and toxic environment of Delhi. Who can ignore the journalism of NDTV's Ravish Kumar that won him the Magsaysay Award? You may disagree with him but definitely cannot ignore him. Or, for that matter, the brave journalism of young television reporter

Tanushree Pandey who stood her ground well past midnight and filmed the forced cremation by insensitive police of a gangraped Dalit girl in Hathras.[29] And how can one ignore the journalists in Kashmir who continue to brave police batons to report on the travails of the troubled Valley?[30] But for every recognition won by a journalist, there are many more who remain unsung and unacknowledged.

My sympathies squarely lie with the very many state reporters who do exceptionally good work but rarely ever get to become top editors. Call it the tyranny of distance, but when it comes to considering candidates for the top job, they mostly go to people who are already working at the publication centres. The state reporters, no matter how good or efficient they are, are constantly overlooked. Making a mark in what is increasingly turning out to be an unremarkable industry is a daunting task. Most of us do not have the wherewithal to market ourselves, unlike a famous but controversial journalist, who hired an international PR agency to do the needful. It has got infinitely more difficult with the polarization that has driven a deep wedge within the media fraternity. If not political loyalty, it is political subservience that is often preferred these days over professional skills.

The *Economist* in one of its recent issues,[31] focused on the threat from the illiberal left and argued that at no other place were the dangers from it more pronounced than in America where the 'liberal' has come to include an illiberal left. Both the liberals and those in the illiberal left want the same things: both believe people should be able to flourish whatever their sexuality or race and both share a suspicion of authority. But as the magazine elaborated, the illiberal left has also brought along a new and unsettling obsession with a narrow vision for obtaining justice, bringing in new tactics to enforce ideological purity. These include not giving platforms to those perceived as enemies and cancelling allies who they believe have transgressed.

I read the particular issue with rapt attention, but felt what it said about the phenomenon in America could be said about present-day India as well. Quintessential liberals like me, caught between the right and the illiberal left, have virtually been left out. Consider this: journalists on the side of the establishment are patronized by those in power. Those against are subjected to hardships, but at least acquire a halo for their courage. They are constantly feted, picking up awards around the globe.

Less in demand are ones like me who are stuck in the middle. Neither for nor against, but with a pronounced preference for both-sides journalism – classic liberal ideals that attach a premium to debates and discussions for ironing out differences – we are generally left stranded. So was the case with *Outlook* during my stint. We were not pro-government. At the same time, we were not considered anti-government enough to be celebrated. Acknowledgement came only when I was sacked and when it suited a particular narrative. 'This is how good editors go missing', tweeted a top journalist ranged against the establishment. For once, I got recognized. But could that be of any solace for someone who suddenly found himself without a job?

7

WEAPONIZATION OF NEWS

THE WORLD SEEMED TO BE ON FIRE THE MOMENT I WOKE UP ONE morning in July 2020. Apart from the very many messages that flooded my phone, it began to ring incessantly from early in the morning. The calls came non-stop, from friends, friends' friends and people who I didn't even know. Also calling were those I was faintly acquainted with. The callers also included politicians – particularly from the Congress party. Though I had little idea what they were talking about, it wasn't difficult to understand that they were mostly angry and aggrieved. Many were distinctly agitated. Some voiced wonderment. How could you do this? What has happened to *Outlook*?

I didn't have an answer straight away. Still groggy and yet to gulp down my morning cup of tea, I felt ambushed without an iota of an idea as to what had hit me. As the messages took me to task and the callers vented their disgust, I attempted to make sense.

Gradually, it all fell in place, and I could gather what the outrage was about. I quickly went online and checked *Outlook*'s website, and then it became abundantly clear what had transpired: As I peacefully slept, an agency story from an automated news feed had gone up on our website. It was about Priyanka Gandhi's bungalow.

That Priyanka Gandhi – the Gandhi scion and general secretary of the party in Uttar Pradesh – had a bungalow in Lutyens' Delhi had escaped my mind. I have never met her in person and had no idea whether she lived there or somebody else lived at the address in her place. I also had no knowledge that the bungalow's allotment to her was about to expire and that she would have had to vacate it shortly. Very ill-informed in matters pertaining to Priyanka Gandhi's bungalow, I began reading the agency story on *Outlook*'s website intently. The phone calls wouldn't stop and were a constant distraction. But I continued reading with the maximum attention I could muster.

A couple of minutes later, I could make sense of what the consternation was about. Indo-Asian News Service (IANS), the news agency, had filed a story under the headline 'PM allows Priyanka Gandhi's request to stay on in Lutyens' bungalow for some time'.[1] *Outlook* had an arrangement going with IANS as a subscriber. They would file news reports which would directly go onto our website without any kind of editing or editorial interference. They were part of an automated news feed. The reports would appear on the website with *Outlook*'s logo on top, and a disclaimer at the bottom, stating that it was part of an automated news feed. IANS would be given credit below as the source of the report.

This report on Priyanka Gandhi's bungalow was no different. It ran under *Outlook*'s name, with the obligatory disclaimer at the bottom. But the damage was done. It was an unmitigated disaster for that matter. Everyone noticed *Outlook*'s name at the top, but most failed to notice the disclaimer below. Very few realized it was an IANS story, and the responsibility for the report was laid squarely on us.

What followed was what is to be expected in a deeply polarized environment. Those in support of the Prime Minister took screenshots of the story that appeared on the *Outlook* website, tweeted massively and took immense pride in what they said was Prime Minister Modi's generosity towards his bitter opponent. Those ranged against Modi suspected foul play and railed against us. Soon, a massive debate swept the social media space, and *Outlook* took centre stage. We found ourselves in the middle of an escalating controversy that we had never bargained for.

In between phone calls that showed no signs of stopping, I hurriedly scrolled through our Twitter timeline and was aghast at what I saw. For every single tweet that praised the report, there were at least four criticizing us for what they felt was partisan reportage. *Outlook* and I, as its editor, were taking a huge battering. Even as I checked the unending stream of tweets, their numbers shot up manifold, and it became an even bigger deluge. Priyanka Gandhi tweeted, using *Outlook*'s screenshot with our logo standing out prominently. She denied the report, insisting she had never requested the Prime Minister for an extension. With the story evidently falling flat, *Outlook* had egg on its face.

Reading the IANS report, I, too, felt it didn't have legs to stand on. It didn't have a quote from Priyanka Gandhi though the report concerned her and her bungalow. It didn't even mention that an attempt had been made by the news agency to reach out to her for her version. On the face of it, the report fell short of what we considered journalistic propriety. And now that Priyanka Gandhi had herself denied the story, *Outlook* was shorn of any defence. Caught off guard by the unseemly controversy, I took to Twitter. I expressed my dismay and disappointment and publicly announced my decision to reconsider *Outlook*'s IANS subscription. 'Ending IANS subscription … Unending disaster,' I wrote in disgust.[2]

There wasn't actually much to reconsider, though. For the purpose of increasing traffic to *Outlook*'s website, the volume – or the number – of stories that we carried every day mattered. The greater the number of stories, the greater the chances of visitors coming on to the site. Boosting online traffic being the objective, the stories that IANS filed helped. It gave us a shot at widening our reach and improving our numbers. Of late, however, several IANS reports had caused us some amount of grief, and I was already on a short fuse when the Priyanka Gandhi episode erupted.

It included a report that the news agency had filed some days earlier on Trinamool Congress MP Mahua Moitra. The enraged MP called me up, bitterly complaining about the story and denying its content. I kept insisting it was an automated feed and we had nothing to do with it. But she was unconvinced. 'Your website carried it, so you are responsible', she maintained at the end of a rather long and difficult conversation.

Yet, I persisted with the IANS automated feed. One, it was an accepted practice by several news websites including the top ones like NDTV. Two, the disclaimer at the bottom that it was an automated feed made me believe that we were adequately covered. But as the Priyanka Gandhi story blew up into a major storm, nothing seemed to matter anymore, and *Outlook* seemed to have run out of pretexts. I well and truly had had enough. Incidentally, just days earlier, we had another big embarrassment because of IANS. The agency had filed a story that again had automatically gone up on our site, saying that the father of Sushant Singh Rajput – the Bollywood actor found dead in his home – had tweeted demanding a CBI enquiry into what was seen by many as his suspicious death.

The fact-checking site, altnews.in, called the bluff. For publicizing its report, IANS had tweeted:[3,4] 'A twitter account of #SushantSinghRajput's father K.K. Singh has surfaced through which he is demanding justice for his son. He has asked for a probe by the CBI.' The IANS tweet quoted the father as saying: 'Today my son Sushant's soul is crying and is demanding an investigation by the #CBI.' But Alt News found the tweet to be fake. 'The tweets were made by an account with the username @K KSingh. This is an impostor account with an earlier username @Real_Aishwarya', it said. In its subsequent report debunking the IANS story, Alt News took a swipe at *Outlook* for publishing fake news. 'Several leading media outlets picked up the story – the *New Indian Express*, *Outlook*, *Mathrubhumi*, *National Herald*, the *Times of India* and the *Pioneer*', Alt News reported.

Stung by the uncharitable coverage for no fault of *Outlook*'s, we flagged it to IANS in an email on 7 July 2020. 'Altnews has done this story', *Outlook*'s email stated, giving out the story link. 'This is damaging to our name … we would like to hear from you on this', the email added. IANS, however, refused to own up to its mistake. Instead, it chose to shift the goalpost. Refusing to delve into the questionable tweet of Rajput's father that its earlier report was based on, IANS, in its reply on the same day, referred to another report it had done, quoting Rajput's cousin and former MLA, Neeraj Kumar Singh, alias Bablu. Headlined 'Chorus grows for CBI inquiry into Sushant's death', the report quoted the cousin as saying, 'the matter should be investigated by the CBI'.[5] He was also quoted as saying, 'Sushant's father K.K. Singh also wants a CBI probe in the case'. According to the IANS email reply, 'His cousin confirms everything'. They refused to retract or apologize for the report that had tainted *Outlook*'s reputation.

It was against this backdrop that the Priyanka Gandhi story happened, and I blew my top. Already aware of the dangers that fake news posed, my alarm bells rang out loudly. That news was being manipulated to suit narratives was not unknown to anyone anymore. Even friends working in other media organizations had been constantly warning me of them. If you watched television news, you were already aware of them, with their script sounding alarmingly similar.

When members of the Tablighi Jamaat turned out to be Covid positive in Delhi at the onset of the pandemic in India, the narratives that were peddled across several channels were just about the same, almost as if they shared the same scriptwriter.[6] TV anchors shook in manufactured rage for days on end over what they termed 'Corona Jihad' by those belonging to a particular minority community.[7] The trend continues to date, and when farmers' protests started over the contentious farm laws, several TV channels in a seemingly choreographed show[8] began raising the bogey of 'Khalistanis infiltrating the protesters' ranks' in unison.[9]

Whatever be the means – subtle or brazen – that news was being meddled with in India was no more a mystery. It was an undeniable reality. The IANS story on Priyanka Gandhi seemed to me to fall in that manipulated category. The story claimed that the PM had, in response to Priyanka Gandhi's request, given her an extension. But Priyanka Gandhi denied it, and there was no immediate evidence that could disprove her denial. In her denial, she wrote:[10] 'This is FAKE NEWS. I have not made any such request to the government. As per the eviction letter handed to me on the 1st of July, I will be vacating the government accommodation at 35 Lodhi Estate by the 1st of August.'

It was never my business to bat for Priyanka Gandhi. If IANS or, for that matter, anyone else had anything against the Congress leader, they were welcome to do an expose on her. That would be legitimate. My point was: a salvo was being fired from *Outlook*'s shoulders, and the salvo seemed to be suspicious in nature. Faced with a barrage of angry calls and annoying messages, I acted quickly. Having tweeted my disappointment with the IANS, I made two calls. The first was to the online editorial team. I told them to update the agency report with Priyanka Gandhi's denial and run it. The second was to our technical support team. I told them to stop forthwith the automated IANS feed and initiate steps to discontinue its subscription.

I thought I had done enough to be on top of a terribly sticky situation and ride out the storm. But I was wrong. Sometime later, a Union minister, who I choose not to name, called. He, in fact, went on to call me at least five times over the next couple of hours. The first question that he posed had me stumped. 'Why did you tweet expressing displeasure over the report?' he pointedly asked. I explained the context, including the issues that we have had recently with IANS. But the minister was unconvinced. 'You shouldn't have', he said, dropping adequate hints that we ought to have let the original report run uncontested. He then followed it up with what could only be described as a bouncer. He suggested that we should not discontinue our IANS subscription.

Thereafter, the minister kept calling every half hour, giving me real-time updates. Hardeep S. Puri, the Union minister for urban affairs, had tweeted thrice, which the minister said proved the story. In the first, Puri wrote:[11] 'Facts speak for themselves! A powerful Congress leader with much clout in the Party called me on 4 July 2020 at 12.05 pm to request that 35, Lodhi Estate be allotted to another INC MP so that Priyanka Vadra can stay on. Let's not sensationalize everything please.'

The spat worsened thereafter. Priyanka Gandhi responded again on Twitter, standing firm on her denial. Responding to the minister's tweet,[12] she wrote: 'If someone called you Mr Puri, I thank them for their concern, and thank you for your consideration as well but it still does not change the facts: I have made no such request and I am making no such request. As I said, I will be vacating the house by the 1st of August.'

Her strong denials notwithstanding, Puri stuck to his guns. An hour later, he tweeted again,[13] this time adding: 'The leader who called me, & many others, is at the very top of the Congress hierarchy … the same political advisor who speaks and acts on your family's behalf. It was when he requested that we decided to give a two-month extension in good faith.' This was followed by another tweet, at 1.46 p.m: 'Would only request you to first sort out these issues within your own party before venting in public. Streak of entitlement & playing victim don't go well together.'

It was evident from the minister's tweets that the IANS story that the *Outlook* website carried wasn't entirely correct. Priyanka Gandhi hadn't requested the government for an extension after all. Going by the minister, it was an aide who approached with the request. The story had drastically changed, and we updated the report further to include the minister's claims and Priyanka Gandhi's denial. Curtly told by the other minister not to discontinue the IANS subscription, we changed our strategy too. We stopped using IANS stories but decided to let the subscription run for the next six months for which we had already paid. It was our way of not earning unwarranted displeasure.

IANS, however, stood its ground. It wouldn't express remorse for any of its recent reports. In an email on 15 July, it defended its track record. 'First, IANS stands by the story "PM allows Priyanka Gandhi's request to stay on in Lutyens' bungalow for some time". It is unfortunate that *Outlook* editor accepted Priyanka Gandhi's denial about the story as the biblical truth without giving IANS a chance to clear its stand after her libelous tweet. That the IANS report was credible has since been verified by the Central government itself', it said.

'The Union minister for Housing and Urban Affairs, Mr Hardeep Singh Puri, in response to Priyanka Gandhi's libelous comment against IANS report, tweeted', the news agency added, citing the tweets by the minister referring to the Congress functionary who reportedly approached. It then went ahead making a rather warped argument:

> The fact that Mr Puri gave exact details of the call of the Congress leader close to Priyanka Vadra, is an indicator that the politician made a request to the government for extension of her stay in the government bungalow, on behalf of Ms Vadra … the Union minister's tweets established that the IANS story was credible and within necessary journalistic parameters. Yet, the *Outlook* Editor, chose to believe Priyanka Vadra and not IANS, a member of its own media fraternity and that

> too, without seeking a clarification from us. The Editor made his presumptuous judgement public, causing damage to the reputation of IANS. The value of the damage is much more than the amount *Outlook* pays for its IANS subscription.

In the IANS reply defending its reports, including the one on Sushant Singh Rajput's father, the news agency turned its attention to Alt News:

> As far as the Altnews fact-checks are concerned, we do regret some of the errors of judgement we have made. But it is strange that *Outlook* gave its quick judgement on IANS based on Altnews, which is a known Leftist-anarchist platform out there to discredit all the non-Left news platforms by clutching at straws. Out of the 2,19,000 stories reported and released by IANS on an average every year ever since our editor Sandeep Bamzai took over, Altnews pointed out three to four stories where our reporters goofed-up out of haste.
>
> But since Altnews is out there to fabricate an optic to paint IANS in a bad light, this negligible percentage of errors that the IANS has made, is being projected as if IANS is the propagator of fake news. IANS has only 75 reporters and 30 editors and yet we generate humongous amount of content, with a margin of error, which is almost nil. But if *Outlook* has decided to turn prejudiced against IANS, because of the reasons known best to your proprietor and editor or because of any political pressure, we at IANS will understand your position.

Though long and righteous in tone, the reply did little to satisfy us. We wrote back with our response, highlighting the concerns that still remained unaddressed. 'We are not questioning IANS's way of operating, functioning or the manner in which it defines journalism. What we are talking about is journalistic propriety and why *Outlook* should be providing a platform for stories of doubtful veracity. The story about Priyanka Gandhi's bungalow is an example. The headline said, "PM allows Priyanka Gandhi's request to stay on in Lutyens' bungalow for some time". But did Priyanka Gandhi make any such request,' our response read.

The story did not back the claim made in the headline and it is a different matter that Ms Gandhi dismissed the story as 'fake', tweeting the automated IANS feed published in *Outlook* and as a result *Outlook* got a bad name for no fault of its own. Tweets later by a Union minister (which the IANS response quotes) said an extension was given on the basis of a request by a senior Congress leader. If that was the case, the headline 'PM allows Priyanka Gandhi's request' was incorrect. If the request was made by someone else on her behalf, the story and the headline ought to have clearly reflected that,' we argued. Resting our case, our reply added:

> Notwithstanding IANS claims [that] the story was correct and within 'journalistic parameters', there is little doubt that both the headline and the story misrepresented facts. The story was also one-sided. Though it dealt with Ms Gandhi, there were no quotes from her, and it is not clear whether any attempts were made to get her version – something that is an integral part of ethical journalism protocol. But *Outlook* is well within its right to decide whether it should offer its platform for such kind of journalism and let its own reputation be tarnished. That this particular story involved a politician is incidental. We have had issues with several IANS stories – some non-political in nature

– in the recent past, putting a big question mark over IANS' trustworthiness.

It cannot be said that the scrap we had over the Priyanka Gandhi story bore any substantive results. IANS never repented and *Outlook* did not renew its subscription when it finally ran out. Fake news, meanwhile, continues to flourish in the country, keeping fact-checking sites such as Alt News busy as never before.

A man is lynched in Guatemala, and it is passed off as Muslims assaulting a man in Goa.[14] Activists critical of the government make a speech and their words are taken out of context and then clipped and edited to convey a wholly different meaning. Pictures are often morphed and used for portraying something else. As mainstream media struggles to stay afloat in the face of sundry challenges including shrinking revenue, fake news seems to have a free run. It remains a big problem for all fair-minded journalists. Credibility and trust in news that we were told are sacrosanct are under siege. Our preoccupation with busting fake news has never ever been such a big priority.

IANS, however, wasn't done with me. A year later, when I was sacked by *Outlook*, it tweeted out[15] part of the termination letter. 'The #Outlook Group has terminated the services of Group Editor-in-Chief Ruben Banerjee (@Rubenbanerjee) with immediate effect for having vitiated the atmosphere and working in an erratic manner', the post read. It followed up by promptly filing a report[16] on the sacking, which was picked up by several dailies and news websites across the country.

The reports were extremely damaging to me. For example, if anyone decides to visit the popular exchange4media website that mostly specializes in news about hirings and appointments at senior levels of the media and advertising industry, they will find a story with my picture prominently proclaiming that I had been sacked.[17] And my digital footprint has also been tainted forever. A Google search of my name now shows up many news reports, courtesy of IANS, about my dismissal from *Outlook*. Evidently, the termination news has overshadowed everything else about me.

I wonder what opinion those reading the reports would form about me. The claims made while sacking me were certainly baseless, levelled with ulterior motives that I can and will unpack bit by bit. IANS, however, wasted no time in putting out the story of my sacking with all the allegations that could be challenged. None from the agency got in touch or sought my version. But then, the IANS story was widely published – from *Dainik Bhaskar* to the *Shillong Times* – and I got a shot at notoriety. Finding myself suddenly unemployed, I comforted myself that any free publicity, after all, is good publicity.

No less a consolation was also the fact that my sullied reputation happened to be just a small collateral damage of what is considered as the dwindling standards of a media beset with complex problems. That it had been a downhill journey for India's media has been well evident for some time. For all its loud, boisterous nature in a marketplace crowded with television channels and publications, that it had been ringing more and more hollow both in terms of credibility and trustworthiness has not been in doubt. Republic TV is a case in point. Irrespective of the controversy it triggered some months ago over its TRP – rigged or not – none can doubt that the channel with its divisive content bordering on toxicity is hugely popular. People tune in every night to watch the channel's celebrated owner-anchor hold a court of his own, delivering sermons and pronouncing instant verdicts. But is it trustworthy? A recent Reuters Institute study let the cat out of the bag, revealing that Republic topped the distrust chart scoring 29 per cent. NDTV, in comparison, was distrusted by 19 per cent of the respondents.[18]

Indian media's storied past provides a measure of its steep fall. Long gone are the times when lofty ideals fired luminaries to launch their newspapers. The *Hindu* was started more than a century ago with an eye to giving an Indian perspective in a media landscape dominated by British voices. Ghanshyam Das Birla financed and later took over *Hindustan Times* to lend support to the nationalist struggle, while Ramnath Goenka's almost fanatical belief in journalism of courage propelled him to launch the *Indian Express*. Similar stellar motives lay behind the launch of most of the other big newspapers – from the now-defunct *Amrita Bazar Patrika* to the *Tribune* that continues to be the preferred choice of a majority of Punjabis.

But the idealism that originally ignited the passion to practise journalism has significantly dimmed over the decades. Newer generations of owners are at the helm of major media houses and many of them are moved by more mundane objectives such as profits and political clout rather than the earlier esoteric goals. As one prominent new-age owner confessed to me rather candidly, a majority of the present-day owners are most likely to wake up every morning these days with the thought of how to make their next Rs 10 crore. Holding the government of the day accountable or making the world a better place to live in have largely receded to being distant thoughts for many of them.

That the goalposts have significantly shifted is borne out by the power structures at many of the media houses. Post liberalization, several of them attempted to corporatize themselves by bringing in outside professionals. But opacity still reigns with many of the media houses continuing to be family-run businesses that account for only a portion of the very large conglomerates they run. Take, for example, the case of *Hindustan Times*. Bequeathed to the current chairperson, Shobhana Bhartia, by her late father, K.K. Birla, the multi-centre daily with a large circulation and lot of influence, happens to be only one of the many businesses that the Bhartias own. Shobhana's husband, Shyam Sunder Bhartia, heads a business empire worth thousands of crores. It includes companies that deal in pharmaceuticals, food, automobile, aerospace and oilfields. And if the close family ties of the Bhartias with the Birlas are to be considered, their interests in businesses multiply manifold.

Diverse business interests that the owners need to protect and promote do not sit well with the idea of a free media. The exact extent of independence that *Hindustan Times* – part of the larger HT Media group – is able to exercise has often been part of public speculation, which further spiralled in the wake of Bobby Ghosh's abrupt exit as the daily's editor-in-chief. But for a few large houses such as the *Times of India*, the *Hindu* or the *Indian Express* for whom media interests remain their mainstay, many others have their fingers in many a pie. Reliance's Mukesh Ambani – India's richest man who is also a media baron owning brands such as Network 18 – is a prime example. Even the owners of *Dainik Bhaskar* – the Hindi daily that surprised everyone with its critical reportage of the second wave of Covid-19 – lord over a business empire that encompasses real estates, textiles and power. The varied interests leave scope for suspicion, prompting some media watchers to even question the true intent behind *Dainik Bhaskar*'s Covid coverage. Critics have pointed out that the paper's reporting – including on episodes such as the Tablighi Jamaat – were far from exemplary. Many, in fact, have accused it of being borderline communal in the recent past.[19]

Quality of journalism is obviously a casualty as media owners do a tightrope walk, balancing the interests of other businesses with that of the news outlets they run. It is not difficult to guess who the winner is in the balancing act. The other businesses are far bigger, and protecting their interests is almost always the foremost priority for most owners. Add to them the new breed of owners behind many of the regional papers and channels, and journalism seems to stand no chance of protecting its autonomy. Flush with the millions they have minted from their mining and other sundry businesses, the media is just a tool for these proprietors to gain access to the corridors of power and wield greater clout.

No matter the motives, being in the media business is a tough proposition in present-day India. The society is polarized, and the space for venting opinion, including dissent, is shrinking. Downgraded from 'free' to 'partly free' by the Washington-based non-profit organization Freedom House,[20] India has also slipped in the Press Freedom Index. It currently stands at a lowly 142 among 180 nations.[21]

The existing landscape exacerbates the troubles for a media that already is besieged on many fronts, including the threat from social media that is swamped by misinformation. The surfeit of fake news should have ordinarily strengthened the position of time-tested journalism built on truthfulness. But under pressure – both political and financial – a significant section of the media itself has fallen for the charm of news that is incorrect but sensational. Sensationalism sells – widening reach, grabbing more advertisements and pleasing those invested in creating a false narrative.

Hastening the media's journey down the slippery slope are the lack of regulations. Article 19 (1) (a) of the Constitution guarantees freedom of expression and speech that has come to be construed as freedom of the press. But there is little regulation in place to ensure that these freedoms are exercised with caution and for the public good. India has regulatory bodies such as the Press Council of India for overseeing its print media, but it remains more of a toothless body with its powers limited to an advisory role. So much so that few take it seriously. Nor did I when, towards the end of my tenure as the *Outlook* editor, the organization was slapped with a Press Council notice for what it deemed to be our violation for publishing an advertisement in the form of news. It's a different matter that the said advertisement that appeared in *Outlook* Hindi was carried under the branding of Outlook Initiative, a standard media practice to distinguish advertisement from news. But the moot point is that the Press Council notice did not alarm me a bit. I just forwarded it to the concerned department, convinced that the press body had no potential to cause us any concrete harm.

Not much harm was done to several television channels either that the National Broadcasting and Digital Standards Authority (NBDSA) found in late 2021 to have erred in airing several 'problematic' programmes the previous year. In a series of strictures, the authority censured channels such as Times Now and Zee News and ordered them to take down videos of several shows that did not meet ethical standards, falsified news and suffered from brazenly communal portrayal of events.[22] The rap on the knuckle that came a year late stopped there. No anchor or reporter was taken to task, and no channel was required to express regret and apologize.

Almost always let off lightly, the media generally remains a loose cannon overwhelmingly preoccupied with sexing up news and seeking to corner as many advertisements as possible. Money made from circulation and subscriptions account for very little of media revenue, forcing most organizations to treat advertisements as their lifeline. They chase them relentlessly, turning the business model more competitive, cut-throat and possibly broken.

It is not the case that advertisements are drying up. According to a report in the *Indian Express*, the advertising industry is set to grow to Rs 70,343 crore by the end of 2022 from Rs 62,577 crore at the end of 2021. But as the report revealed, more and more advertisers prefer to advertise in the digital medium, which is set to grow to Rs 23,673 crore by 2022 compared to Rs 18,938 crore by the end of 2021. The digital advertising pie holds out tantalizing prospects for profits, prompting a proliferation of digital outlets. Many legacy media organizations have also plunged into the online space with manic zeal, hoping for rich harvests.

But as Rajesh Mahapatra, the former editor-at-large at *Hindustan Times*, who once was the guiding force behind the daily's online push puts it, the legacy media's tryst with digital has generally been disappointing. Having entered the digital news environment with considerable assets – such as credibility, audience loyalty and newsroom capabilities – the returns against the investment remain remarkably low with technological giants such as Google and Facebook walking away with most of the moolah. Armed with complex algorithms that determine the discoverability of news sites and news, they have acquired the power to dictate how content is disseminated. That has contributed to growing polarization and promotion of particular narratives, besides entirely skewing the revenue sharing arrangement for advertisements.

The same *Indian Express* report highlighted the alarming imbalance that has come to define Indian media organizations' relationship with the tech giants such as Google that, incidentally, is headed by Sundar Pichai, an Indian. The report[23] stated that the combined advertisement revenue of Google and Facebook is higher than the combined advertisement revenue of the top ten listed traditional media companies. The tech giants made Rs 23,213 crore against Rs 8,396 crores made by the media houses. Zee Entertainment Enterprises, with the largest market capitalization among the listed identities, was reported to have earned Rs 3,710 crore from advertisement revenue, compared to Rs 9,326 crore by Facebook India and Rs 13,887 crore by Google India for 2020-21.

The disparity in sharing of the dough has piled further pressure on media's already broken business model. The consequences had to show up in various ways, and they are on display currently in the shape of dwindling credibility, ever-desperate commercialization and rising sensationalism. So, does the media in India have any future left?

Anant Goenka, the young executive director of the Indian Express group and grandson of the legendary Ramnath Goenka, acknowledged that the situation was distressing. But what he didn't seem to agree with me, during a free-wheeling conversation, was that the reality had descended into being dire.

'Of course, there are new challenges but at the *Indian Express*, we have dealt with the dire. You can say the Emergency was our vaccine; it has built our immunity, maybe this is our booster shot. You can still do your journalism if you wish to', he insisted.

> Unfortunately, social media has made it seem that a smartly expressed opinion is great reporting when you and I know it is not. That's why we continue to deeply invest in a 300-plus newsroom with the finest investigative reporters and editors in the country. From Panama Papers and the ICICI-Chanda Kochhar or Cox and Kings investigation to Jan Dhan accounts

> being inflated, the misuse of draconian security laws, purchase of land near Ram temple, fudging of Covid testing records in Bihar, or how cyclone relief in West Bengal went to those close to the ruling party, we have done some of our best work in these challenging times. So this means we get angry and, sometimes, threatening phone calls from everyone, but our editors, our managers, know how to handle these calls. That's our history. And maybe that's why, at least I hope that's why, those in power, irrespective of their political hue, still take our questions. Because they know we listen to all, with an open mind; we have no favourites.

According to him, this is what helps *Express* live up to its tagline of 'journalism of courage,' its steadfast belief in objectivity. 'We pull no punches and call spade a spade', he added. It does not necessarily earn them accolades and those ranged against the establishment were particularly annoyed when, for example, the newspaper reported that accusations of murder shrouding the death[24] of judge Brijgopal Harkishan Loya were without merit. Judge Loya[25] dealt with cases relating to the Central Bureau of Investigation, including the suspicious death of Sohrabuddin Sheikh that, many believed, implicated Union Home Minister Amit Shah,[26,27] who happened to be the home minister in Gujarat then. Loya died in December of 2014 and many, including sections of the media, speculated for months on end about foul play in his sudden demise.

'We report freely because we are neither pro-government nor anti-government. No media group would touch the Panama Papers except us because, one, we know how to take pressure and, two, we have no business other than the journalism business. We are pro-truth and given that truth will always be contested, we are pro-fairness, pro-accuracy. I think that's what pro-nation and pro-democracy mean', Goenka said. He stressed that the *Express* was not in the political game to prop up or try to bring down any government unlike several media houses now and was, therefore, committed to providing a space for all voices.[28]

'The *Express* Adda is our event for listening to newsmakers and our guest list reflects the richness of Indian discourse. We have hosted riveting exchanges with Dr Amartya Sen and Arvind Kejriwal and with Yogi Adityanath and Smriti Irani. And each one a blockbuster. And why not? We will be failing in our duty if we don't do this', Goenka added.

How difficult is it to remain objective and still survive in a market polarized and patronized selectively? 'Well, it's not easy, we won't be making the Fortune 500 lists any time soon, but stay the course whatever the noise, work hard 24/7 to keep our credibility and don't get greedy. Searching for truth in polarized democracies may not be a great revenue model but, as my grandfather and my father have shown, it is worth betting everything on', the heir to the Goenka media stable signed off on a hopeful note.

8

THE ENDGAME

S. Mulgaonkar, B.G. Verghese, Arun Shourie, N. Ram, Chitra Subramaniam, Aswhini Sarin... We were never short of either hope or role models when we were coming of age as journalists. All of them were big names with bigger exploits to boot. Mulgaonkar and Verghese were editors par excellence with stellar reputations. Arun Shourie, at the peak of his popularity, shone brightly like no one else. As the uncompromising editor of the *Indian Express* that prided itself for practising 'journalism of courage', he had caught the popular imagination by running a no-holds-barred campaign against Rajiv Gandhi over the controversial Bofors arms deal. Shourie wrote scathing pieces and his fame further soared. Tremendously erudite and a wordsmith, his pieces were something that the nation anxiously awaited to appear on the *Express* front page.

Then, there was N. Ram of the *Hindu*, who, together with the paper's Geneva correspondent, Chitra Subramaniam, was also at the forefront of the aggressive media coverage on Bofors. Some Rs 60 crore were allegedly paid to middlemen in the arms deal, and the Ram-Subramaniam duo provided much of the fodder that ultimately sank Rajiv Gandhi's government in the late 1980s.[1] What Ashwini Sarin did was also unforgettable. As an *Indian Express* reporter, he had bought a young woman, Kamla, from a flesh market in Dholpur at the tri-junction of Rajasthan, Uttar Pradesh and Madhya Pradesh, and blown the lid off a flourishing sex-trafficking racket. It was made into a film, cementing Sarin's cult status.[2]

Fed on a constant diet of heroic exploits by the then top journalists, we had a wide cast of role models to choose from. Their no-nonsense style of journalism was part of folklore and we, at our young impressionable ages, fawned over them. The list was long and illustrious, and it included Dileep Padgaonkar, who rose to become the editor of the country's biggest newspaper chain, the *Times of India*. The positions they held and the work they did were important and awe-inspiring. Padgaonkar himself famously said so once. 'I have the second-most important job in the country – after that of the prime minister', he was quoted as saying.[3] What he said got him instant public attention, but it seemingly wasn't much appreciated by the *Times* management which soon started clipping the wings of the editorial team. If insiders at the media behemoth are to be believed, editors there have become showpieces with marketing and advertisement personnel of the paper calling the shots.

But back then, I was star-struck. The editors and journalists who dominated the scene were larger than life and were definitely worth emulating. It never crossed my mind that I could become an editor like them. Their boots were too big to step into, their fabled exploits too daunting to match. Forget their achievements, I couldn't even dream of undergoing the inglorious, high-voltage exits that some of them were subjected to.

As is the case now, editors in the past too were hostage to the diktats of powerful newspaper owners. Perhaps, they had more character and were people with stronger consciences, but they still had to contend with proprietors who had minds of their own. The Jains of the *Times of India* had unmatched clout; the Birlas of *Hindustan Times* had their interests to protect; and the mercurial Ramnath Goenka of the *Indian Express* had his own ideas about running the newspaper he owned.

This meant the editors often fell foul of the paper barons and lost jobs just as unceremoniously as they do now. The manner of their sacking was messy at times and perhaps as dramatic as the lives they led. Occasionally, the terminations too became as legendary as the legends themselves. For instance, an editor left the office for lunch, only to find on returning that his nameplate had been removed and his room locked. Another editor was told to vacate his chair without notice since his successor had arrived.

Following a little more than a three-year stint as *Outlook*'s editor without much to complain about for most of it, I definitely wasn't prepared for a similar ending. The going was good, though the money was not even a patch of what other top names in the profession made. I, in fact, made a virtue of the low pay, proudly positioning myself among my tight-knit circle of friends as perhaps 'the cheapest editor' in the country. But what the position of *Outlook*'s editor provided me was immeasurable in terms of money. To be one of Vinod Mehta's successors was a huge high. To edit a magazine of the stature of *Outlook*, which commanded instant respect and recognition, was also an honour.

However, the first strains souring the otherwise smooth stint showed up following the 'Missing' cover. Tempers were temporarily frayed, and tensions rose internally in the immediate aftermath of the issue. But advised to strategically lie low, I ducked, and it seemed the storm had passed. We got back to work and carried on as if nothing was amiss. Some two months later, I was promoted again – the third time in three years that my role had been expanded.

Having joined the *Outlook* English magazine as the editor in 2018, I became its editor-in-chief in 2019. The next year, in 2020, I took over as the editor-in-chief of two other group magazines – *Outlook Money* and *Outlook* Hindi. Then again, in July 2021, I was made the group editor-in-chief, responsible for the rest of the magazines from the stable, including *Outlook Traveller* and *Outlook Business*. I also headed the digital verticals of the group, giving me an unparalleled high. Given my career graph, I guess I could be forgiven for at times feeling self-important.

But my journey from being 'important' to a virtual nobody didn't take long. Days after the latest promotion, *Outlook* carried the cover story on the 'Tyranny of Terror Laws' alongside the story on the Pegasus snooping controversy and the latent tensions that bubbled in the immediate aftermath of the 'Missing' cover resurfaced. I was curtly told the choice of stories was not to the liking of those who mattered.

Communication with the management turned terse and testy, as evidenced when Viren Raheja, the younger son of *Outlook* promoter-patriarch Rajan Raheja, joined me on a conference call one day with CEO Indranil Roy. The call stretched for a long time, but it quickly became crystal clear that we were no longer on the same page. We agreed on several scores but also disagreed on some. Viren talked about what we had been discussing within the company for some time – adopting a digital-first strategy. There was general agreement that print publications were no longer profitable propositions, with the cost of production outstripping revenue. Advertisements were moving away to other platforms, and persisting with our focus on print didn't make much business sense anymore. Viren rightfully pushed for embracing the transformation unfolding across media and made a strong case for adopting digital as the principal focus. A younger generation of readers, he said, was consuming news on their mobiles and tablets and we needed to adapt to the changing tastes and habits of those we catered to. Print was passe, he stressed.

Having spent no less than twelve years with Al Jazeera's digital vertical, I readily agreed. I understood the power and reach of online news. As a matter of fact, I had in an official email welcomed *Outlook*'s planned digital push, but with a few caveats. I underscored that we should protect our quality of journalism going forward. It meant that we keep producing quality magazines and go onto the digital space with premium content that would help us stand out from the clutter. Our 'differentiator' content should thereafter be bolstered with better technology, product and steps to improve our social media discoverability.

With our cutting-edge magazine content serving as the core, we could then ramp up online coverage and add more elements such as audio and video to grab more eyeballs. To me, *Outlook* with the right approach could be in a win-win situation. Viren, however, didn't share my enthusiasm. He talked about how Dhirubhai Ambani had once 'disrupted' his business model to reinvent

Reliance and insisted we also needed to go in for disruptions. In other words, it meant we could let the quality of our print magazines decline while we focused more on digital.

Reporters' top priority would be to file stories for online and the magazines could make do with stories they managed to file in their spare time. The suggestion seemed to me to be akin to committing hara-kiri. The very idea that we would bring out magazines that compromised on quality did not exactly sound exciting. Also, I feared that *Outlook* would lose its reputation minus the quality journalism that it stood for. It would become ordinary, and no matter how much we tried or invested in digital, our efforts wouldn't pay off.

Viren seemed to have already made up his mind and insisted that *Outlook*'s reporters start filing at least three stories a day for online. I thought it was an absurd idea and told him so. Credible stories take research and leg work, and it is virtually impossible to manufacture them by the hour. A quota of three per day would mean forcing reporters to rewrite press releases, which, when posted online, would make no difference in carving out our niche in the digital space. It would also spell doom for the magazines since the reporters – we only had a limited number of them – would begin to ignore quality for quantity.

I kept stressing the need to strike the right balance between our print and digital needs while Viren stuck to ramping up the volume of stories to be filed for online. This was the first time that the management was directly pushing the *Outlook* editorial team towards a path it must take, and the conversation that stretched for nearly an hour turned stressful. My hand had been forced, and I took Viren's suggestion to the staff. They overwhelmingly shot it down as being impractical. Instead of three a day, they said they could at best try and file four stories a week for online publication. What they said would have made sense to anyone with knowledge of editorial matters, as it did to me. What I didn't understand at that point in time was that my inability to deliver on the number of stories would cost me dearly. I would be viewed as an obstructionist.

This was bolstered no less than a week later.

In an email which I possess, the CEO now insisted that we retrench staff from the *Outlook* main magazine, complaining bitterly that retrenchments that we had already carried out in other verticals had still not brought down costs to the desired level. He then went on to give me some names who he felt I should let go forthwith. What the CEO now asked for was something I couldn't accept.

I was alarmed. At least some of the names on the chopping block were *Outlook*'s best reporters, and there was no way I could ask them to leave. One was Ajay Sukumaran, a correspondent based in the capital of a southern state, who wrote extremely well. His work, which included several well-researched cover stories, was outstanding, and I simply couldn't imagine showing him the door. In an email reply that I wrote to the CEO the next day, I agreed only partially – that it was okay to let go of an elderly staff member who had retired and was on extension. About the rest, I said a firm 'No'. My email on 28 July 2021 was short and pointed. 'Dear Indranil, there are things that I will not do, and they include not sacking journalists who are good', it read.

In contrast to the first three years of my time in *Outlook*, during which we worked together as allies, a gulf now unmistakably widened between me and the CEO, who sat in a room that was right across from mine. Our meetings became infrequent, and we progressively talked less. Though there was never ever a big argument or a fight, I could feel the tension building – first and majorly over the type of content we could do and then over online strategy and the proposed sackings. Though somewhat perturbed, my alarm bells had still not started ringing, and I was naïve to think that the irritants between me and the management would be ironed out over time. But it didn't, and the changed reality blew up in my face soon thereafter.

It started innocuously with meetings that the CEO began to have independently with certain editorial members who reported to me. On the agenda was the revamp of websites of group magazines, and I presumed I was not being kept in the loop with the purpose of not overburdening me. My plate was already full with five print magazines and work related to the websites. Then, matters swiftly took a serious turn. The CEO decided to speak to the digital head directly and discuss a few things. But the discussion got heated, and an argument broke out.

The digital head was extremely agitated and called me late at night to tell me what had transpired. He then sent in his resignation over email. I decided to sit on it, reasonably certain I could broker a settlement the next day when tempers had cooled down. I thought I had the luxury of time since the digital head reported to me and I was supposed to decide what to do with his resignation. But when I woke up the next morning, I found the CEO had already accepted his resignation. Saubhagya Kala was made redundant overnight.

I attempted to quickly find a replacement and interviewed someone. I then suggested that she be hired on a three-months' probation. But in what was to be a rarity in matters relating to editorial within *Outlook*, the CEO wanted to speak to her himself. He did so and rejected her. Informing me about his decision in an email, he then went on to name his choice as the replacement: a new staff member hired for a limited role just three days earlier. That was unusual since editorial decisions were considered the domain of the editor-in-chief alone. I didn't agree with the choice for several reasons, including that the person the CEO rooted for had a different set of expertise and had never worked on the general news desk. Even her temperament to head a team was untested. 'The person doesn't understand politics', I wrote. 'The person doesn't need to', the CEO responded. While we vehemently disagreed, one thing was clear: the CEO had begun to call the shots.

That I was being undercut and undermined was now beyond doubt. Several more emails were exchanged between me and the CEO and I once again raised my old concerns – about content, the absurd demands for three stories a day and the pressure to sack more people – and waited for a response. When none came, I followed up with another mail intimating to the CEO that I would go on a month's leave from the day after.

'I would attend office tomorrow and at the end of the working day would inform the rest of the staff that I am going on leave', I wrote on 10 August 2021. As the editor-in-chief, I never in the past had to seek his approval for going on leave. Of course, I kept him in the loop and this time, too, was no different. However, the CEO did not respond to my mail – he neither approved nor rejected – and I went to work the next day and, as promised, wrote an email to the editorial staff that I was going on leave. 'I am going on leave for a month from tomorrow. I will be in Delhi, but would prefer not to take any calls – at least for the first few days. Stay well and stay safe', I wrote to my team before leaving the office for what turned out to be the last time.

Calls nevertheless started pouring in soon after I returned home. Senior members of the editorial staff began enquiring what had gone wrong and whether it had anything to do with our 'Missing' cover or the other cover stories we had done later. Soon, the word about my sudden departure spread and reporters from several news organizations began reaching out to check on what they were hearing. Among them was a reporter from Newslaundry, a hugely popular media website. I evaded the queries initially but confirmed later that I had indeed proceeded on leave to 'clear my head and contemplate'. I deliberately kept my statement short and vague.

A day later, Newslaundry carried very prominently a story[4] headlined 'Is *Outlook* editor Ruben Banerjee being pushed out for a cover criticizing the government?' The story speculated about the reasons behind my sudden leave and touched upon very many other aspects of *Outlook*'s operations, including the story we had done on Pegasus and issues related to delayed salaries for staff. The report quoted current and past employees, including Indranil. He had some interesting things to say. Asked if I was leaving the company, he said, 'Not at all. I had approved his leave … There's been a lot of work going on and Ruben said, "let me take a break",' he elaborated. He also denied that there had been any pressure on the management after the 'Missing' cover. On the issue of Pegasus not making it as a cover story, he said: 'We had this discussion and found that there was nothing new in the report.'

A footnote at the bottom of the Newslaundry report now states that the story has been updated with a clarification on salaries that Indranil later provided them with. He, however, never disputed or denied the quote about 'approving' my leave. So, I remained on leave, reading books, watching web series, and taking long aimless walks around my neighbourhood. Two days later – on 15 August 2021 – Indranil messaged that he wished to speak to me. He called and enquired whether 'I would return to work after my leave', saying the *Outlook* promoters wanted to know what my plans were.

The phone conversation was short, and the line of questioning strange. I asked him whether he was ever asked if he would come back as and when he went on leave. He didn't answer, and I also did not deem it fit to answer what I thought was a very inappropriate question. As far as I was concerned, I was simply on leave, and that was it. Some ten days later, on 30 August 2021, I had a long chat with Akshay Raheja, Rajan Raheja's eldest son. I shared all my concerns, and he heard me out patiently. He then promised to process all that information and get back. But more than a week passed, and I still waited. With my month's leave shortly getting over and suffering from a bout of seasonal flu and fluctuating blood pressure, I had to do something. I wrote an email to Indranil, copying Akshay Raheja, seeking an extension of my leave. There began an exchange of emails again, which read sequentially, tells the full story of how matters soon reached a sordid end.

It began with my email on 8 September 2021. It read:

> Dear Indranil,
>
> This is to inform that I am not well. I am suffering from several ailments and would therefore like to extend my month's leave that expires on September 12. I hope to keep you updated on the progress I make.
>
> While I convalesce, I would like to get clarity on certain work-related issues that have caused me immense concern. They are as follows:
>
> You have in the recent past repeatedly told me that we cannot any more freely write on news events. You particularly

had objections to one of our recent cover stories on the Tyranny of Terror Laws. You also expressed reservations about our reportage on the Pegasus controversy. While I am convinced that we had never lost sight of our balanced and objective style of journalism, covering all sides of any given story, what you told me has put me in a quandary. I would like you to shed more light on what exactly you have in mind and clear my doubts. I am certain you wouldn't suggest anything that goes against unbiased journalism and jeopardises *Outlook*'s existence as a credible news magazine.

I would also appreciate clarity on the way things are run currently. Just before I went on leave, you chose to directly speak to our digital editor and reportedly had some disagreement. The digital editor sent in his resignation which you accepted without consulting me. I thereafter recommended someone who in my view could hold the fort in his place, but you rejected it without explaining the reasons. Thereafter, you held consultations with some of my editorial staff behind my back and zeroed in on someone for overseeing our digital operations. As the chief editor, I voiced my concern but you paid no heed.

I believe the same practice of undermining me continues. Several members of the staff have put in their papers, and you have accepted them unilaterally. I understand several new editorial appointments have also been made by you, but surprisingly, I have not been kept in the loop. That you have not extended the basic courtesy of either consulting me or getting my approval on editorial hires is something that I find extremely disrespectful. I am the Group Editor-in-Chief responsible for all editorial decisions, but your recent actions have undoubtedly undercut my authority and position. I would like to know what made you act unilaterally and where does it leave the editor-in-chief? As and when I get well and resume my duties, will I have any authority left? Or will it be you who will run editorial operations? If the latter is the case, what will be the role of the Group Editor-in-Chief?

While there are other issues that we need to discuss, the above mentioned two are the ones that are on top of my mind now. They need your immediate attention and clarification for the good of the organization.

I hope to hear from you, while I recover from my spell of ill-health.

Thanking you,
Ruben Banerjee

Indranil replied on 11 September 2021, but now chose to accuse me of going on 'unbefitting' leave. He also did not directly address the concerns I had raised.

Dear Rubenda,

In its 26 years of existence, *Outlook* has always stood for fair editorial practices and is well-known for it. You have not only witnessed the same in the last three years but have been an advocate of the freedom and fairness that you, as Editor, have enjoyed at *Outlook*.

As you are aware *Outlook* has embarked on its digital journey and our mandate is to build a robust digital medium and team. In the middle of our attempts to aggressively promote *Outlook*'s digital media platform, your unbefitting decision to go on a month-long leave left me in dire straits to handle the difficult phase. The vacuum and uncertainty caused in the organization by your month-long leave was threatening to affect our print and digital operations. Our renewed efforts to bolster, improve and push the digital medium could not have been postponed or compromised. I was constrained to take many decisions, including recruitments, all of which were in the interest of the organization. I hope you appreciate the fact that these explanations are offered in our tradition of fairness.

As the CEO, I have always acted in the interest of the organization.

I sincerely wish you had sat across the table and ironed out your concerns with me.

Best Regards,
Indranil

Within hours of receiving his reply, I responded, giving concrete examples of how I had been undercut and undermined. I also asked how and why he had told Newslaundry that he had 'approved' my leave when he was accusing me now of going on 'unbefitting' leave. I also posed a few pertinent questions on his statement on Pegasus.

Dear Indranil,

Thanks for finally bothering to respond to my email, even though your reply is a poorly drafted attempt to distract from the core issues raised by me over the past one month.

That *Outlook* has been a beacon of free, fair journalism for the past 26 years was never the bone of contention. The issues raised by me – about pressure not to report freely and interference in editorial matters – are a recent phenomenon. They arose only after a particular *Outlook* cover story in May this year.

I first flagged my concerns to you in emails on 10 August, expressing my dismay at your brazen attempts to undermine me and interfere in editorial matters. You rather unnecessarily got into an argument with the digital editor and when he sent his resignation, you accepted it unilaterally. The said editor reported to me, and only I as the group editor-in-chief, should have decided what to do with his offer to resign.

I was not on leave when you accepted the resignation and when you rejected my subsequent recommendation for a quick replacement. I was also not on leave when you, as you have admitted in one of your email replies during the exchanges we had on 10 August, decided to engage with a recently hired staff directly and concluded that she should take charge of our digital vertical. You did this all behind my back, and I shared my concerns – including the pressure not to report freely – as early as on 10 August.

Should you require, I can send you the emails to jog your failing memory.

In your bid to obfuscate, you in your reply have said that I went on an 'unbefitting' long leave which has left you in dire straits.

But the fact is I intimated to you my decision to go on leave at 10.10 p.m. on 10 August. In the email, I told you I would intimate the staff only the next day. You chose not to reply to my email. In fact, you never replied.

However, you told the web portal www.newslaundry.com later that 'you have approved my leave'. Though the said story has now been updated with a clarification which you sought to give them later over *Outlook* salaries, you never disputed the quote of yours that you have approved my leave. In light of the quote, you must decide whether you approved or did not approve my leave.

You also self-incriminated yourself in the same Newslaundry story while commenting on the Pegasus controversy. 'We had this discussion and found that there was nothing new in the report', you told the Newslaundry reporter. Really – nothing new in the report? Scores of prominent citizens are reportedly under surveillance, and you dismiss it as nothing new? And under what authority? Were you already interfering in editorial matters?

While I look forward to hearing from you again, I hope you would be more truthful in future, and address the real issues instead of side-stepping them.

Best wishes.
Ruben Banerjee

Indranil replied on 12 September 2021.

Dear Rubenda,

I am in receipt of your email, and I only wish to say that I completely disagree with your perception of what has transpired between us.

I would not want to be dragged into an exchange of communication on the subject at this point. Currently I am stressed in respect of resources and therefore we have recruited an editor for *Outlook* who will be joining us soon.

We can discuss all the issues when we meet in person next, after you recover.

Best Regards,
Indranil

Not getting any substantial clarifications from the CEO, I wrote back the same day, stating that I wasn't surprised that an editor for *Outlook* has been hired without even consulting the group editor-in-chief.

Dear Indranil,

Your latest, self-incriminating email confirms your continued brazen undermining and undercutting of my authority. That you don't wish to engage with me on the issues that I raised any further is also understandable. The documented evidence – I can furnish all the emails – is stacked against you, and you have no other option but to fall back on plain bluster.

Going by what you have been doing, it does not surprise me anymore that you have gone ahead and appointed an editor for *Outlook* without even consulting the Group Editor-in-Chief.

By the way, *Outlook* was not exactly rudderless or headless while I have been on leave. There is a Managing Editor and an Executive Editor. Your act of surreptitiously hiring an editor shows your utter lack of respect for senior editorial staff.

In any case, I reserve the right of revisiting your decision should I find the new editor wanting in any way once I resume duties after I have fully recovered.

Ruben Banerjee

Three days after Indranil wrote that 'we can discuss all issues face-to-face when you recover', I recovered from my ill health. Feeling fit on the morning of 15 September 2021, I decided to rejoin and wrote an email stating so. The email was also copied to the HR manager and Akshay Raheja.

Dear Indranil,

This is to inform you I am resuming duty today. I am feeling much better now.

Looking forward to picking up from where I had left, though I must say I am greatly disappointed and dismayed that I have not been officially intimated the name of the new editor of *Outlook*, who has been hired without my knowledge. I came to know about the name from news reports.

It's baffling that even basic courtesies and niceties have deserted *Outlook*'s management. But this was to be expected I think, given your attempts to humiliate me in recent months.

Anyways, I would request Sashi and Alka to ask housekeeping to get my room cleaned and properly sanitised. I hope to see you in office.

Best
Ruben Banerjee

Raring to go, I shot off messages on *Outlook*'s internal WhatsApp groups and an email to the editorial staff, informing them that I was back. I welcomed the new *Outlook* editor and suggested a cover story on Yogi Adityanath of Uttar Pradesh and his recent controversial 'Abba Jaan' statement for the next issue.

A detailed story brief followed, and it read:

Abba Jaan & Adityanath. As crucial UP elections draw near, it's clear there will be more communal polarisation. Yogi Adityanath's PR machinery is already on top gear – despite the *Express* ad fiasco – and he is being marketed as UP's Vikash Purush. Simultaneously, his communal pitch is getting sharper: Abba Jaan, ATS Darul Uloom Deoband, the talk of safety of cows, etc. Next year's UP elections are crucial and is of immense interest to everyone – young and old.

Yogi's controversial Abba Jaan comment has given us a great hook to look at Uttar Pradesh and what's in store. Let's make the most of it for 'the fully loaded news magazine', my story brief concluded, detailing the elements our next issue must have for a well-rounded objective coverage.

Topicality being the cornerstone of any weekly magazine, it was a perfect and timely cover to do. Some messages and calls immediately followed from some staff members. They were glad I was back and welcomed my story idea. But then, an hour later, they began panicking. Apparently, instructions had gone out to remove me from *Outlook* WhatsApp groups, and I began to be removed from them one by one. Soon came an email from the CEO, terminating my services.

Dear Rubenda,

Unfortunately, on 11 August 2021, you informed your colleagues that you would not be accessible as you were going on a month-long leave. On 8 September 2021, you wrote to me that you are not well and would want to extend your leave, without indicating any timeline. Suddenly today morning, I received your email stating that you are resuming work effective today. I wish to bring to your notice that despite discussing and agreeing to tight timelines with a view to consolidate operations into one-newsroom and launch the new website in the first week of September 2021, your abrupt absence from work left *Outlook* stressed.

As CEO I think it will not augur well for the discipline and the future of the organization even as you choose to continue in this erratic manner. The correspondence exchanged and your conduct have completely vitiated the atmosphere.

Therefore, I write to inform you that I am compelled to terminate your contract with Outlook Publishing (India) Limited with immediate effect as per the terms of your agreement.

A formal letter will be sent to you. I am asking HR to get in touch with you to complete the exit formalities.

I wish you all the best in your future endeavours.

Best Regards,
Indranil Roy

I stood summarily sacked. Having gone on record earlier that he had 'approved' my leave, and three days after writing that 'we can discuss the issues face-to-face after you recover', the CEO chose to dismiss me since 'my abrupt absence from work left *Outlook* stressed'. Since the time I decided to go on leave and returned, I had written just two emails to the staff – one to tell them I was going on leave, and the other to inform them that I was back. I had sent no other SMSs or written any WhatsApp messages to the team. But the CEO, in his email terminating my services, accused me of 'vitiating' the atmosphere and 'erratic conduct'. Courtesy IANS, it soon turned into a public spectacle.

More in-depth coverage of my abrupt sacking followed, and they were largely sympathetic. '*Outlook* Group Editor-in-Chief sacked 2 hours after rejoining work and commissioning cover on Yogi', said the headline in The Print.[5] '*Outlook*'s "Missing" editor gets the sack after spate of anti-Modi government stories', read the headline in thefederal.com[6]. Newsclick.in did a detailed story, headlined 'What led to *Outlook* editor's exit?'[7], while Newslaundry's report proclaimed: 'Why did *Outlook* get a new editor and sack Ruben Banerjee?'[8]

The reports made pertinent points: How could I be sacked for going on leave when the CEO had himself said he had approved it; or how could I have vitiated the atmosphere when I had not written anything to the staff instigating them? As and when the reporters sought my views, I said whatever I had to say. Indranil was quizzed too, and he continued giving his spin. He even found fault with the fact that I had suggested a cover story idea on joining. 'Staff were already working on a story when Ruben came up with his idea', he said.

What he did not say is that in dynamic newsrooms, stories kept changing constantly. *Outlook* has in the past changed its cover stories as late as on Wednesday mornings – the day when the magazine goes to print. In this case, I was suggesting a story with more than a week to go for the deadline. In any case, the choice of the cover lay vested with the editorial team and not the CEO. Indranil also did not elaborate on the 'tight timelines' that my going on leave had apparently jeopardized. For that matter, no such timelines were ever shared with me – either verbally or in any emails.

The termination knocked off in a trice whatever trace of self-importance I may have acquired over the years. I was unequivocally shown to be a paper tiger without teeth and claws, who survived only at the pleasure of the promoters. It, in more ways than one, held up a mirror to the myriad problems our noble profession confronted, more than ever. Editors and journalists lost jobs in the past too. But they were not half as endangered as they are now. The ranks of owners then had people such as Ramnath Goenka. But increased competition in the media space and shrinking revenues have ostensibly multiplied the pressures on promoters who now attach a greater premium on balance sheets of companies they run. They are more dependent on governments – at the Centre and states – for survival. The intermittent raids on the premises of several media houses have also put real fear in many of them.

This is not to suggest that all these are only of recent making or a post-2014 phenomenon. They happened earlier too, and Vinod Mehta, in one of his best-selling books,[9] narrated how the Rahejas themselves had suffered during the reign of Atal Bihari Vajpayee following *Outlook*'s expose on influence-peddling in the PMO by a trio of influential people that included the Prime Minister's son-in-law. Raids followed on *Outlook* premises across the country and the Rahejas were harassed for months on end.[10] They would be ceaselessly made to do the rounds of offices of the investigating agencies and forced to wait. The situation has got infinitely worse since then, and few now have the stomach to suffer such ignominies.

Most media houses have grown risk-averse and prefer to play safe, defanging journalists and editors for the purpose of buying peace. That the media has lost much of its earlier influence is clear from the fact that Prime Minister Modi hasn't felt it necessary to hold a press conference or field unchoreographed questions from them even once in his unfinished tenure to date. He chooses to use social media for his messaging and connecting with the people.

As and when he volunteers to be interviewed, the interview is done by sections of the media that are unabashedly loyal. They lob easy questions – such as the now infamous '*So much hua hai, kitna kiya hai…aur kya bacha hai!*' asked by a TV anchor during an interview.[11] Hard follow-up questions are invariably never asked. With big media having all but lost its appetite to stand up, it is up to the small, no frills-attached news outlets such as The Print, The Wire, Scroll, Newsminute and Newslaundry, to step in. They have no sundry business interests to protect and hence are better placed to face the pressures that are exerted these days. Both their legacy and reach could be limited, but they are better placed to shoulder the responsibility of pursuing brave journalism like no one else.

My termination was also an occasion for pent-up emotions to be freely vented – both for and against. A talented senior colleague whom I had promoted within the first week of my joining *Outlook* wrote an enormous essay[12] for a periodical seeking to appropriate most of the credit for the journalism we did. In doing so, he praised and diminished me in parts. Detractors, including some who I never realized hated me, were far less charitable. 'What goes around comes around', messaged a senior whose column in *Outlook* digital we had to discontinue because we couldn't pay outside contributors anymore. A few former colleagues sent outright abusive messages while the cake for the most downright below-the-belt hit job went to one Sajjan Kumar Singh. Using a news report of my sacking that prominently showed my photograph, he posted on Facebook[13]: 'Such fixers in the garb of journalism have many friends to do his bidding. Having peddled the narrative for a BJP leader from Odisha in 2018 by writing a nasty biography on Naveen Patnaik without a single source … he went on to do a volte face post-Bengal mandate by going after the BJP in more radical ways than even the likes of *Caravan*, perhaps under the assumption that power equation in Uttar Pradesh and by extension in 2024 would be changing. All the while the magazine suffered colossally in every sense under his editorship. A failed editor with a penchant for bidding for xyz than doing journalism is playing the victim and his friends from the fraternity are shedding liberal tears.'

The foul comments, fortunately, though, were outnumbered by compliments that came my way. The shortest and the sweetest was from Sumita Mehta, Vinod Mehta's wife. 'Great respect for you Ruben', she messaged in the days after my dismissal. 'When one window closes, many others will open. Trust me you will see that happen soon.' 'Tipping my hat to you', wrote a fellow journalist. 'Proud to know you', wrote another. They lifted my spirits at a time when I was down and out. Suddenly left with a lot of spare time, I ruminated over the past and contemplated the future.

I was moved to tears when a young colleague at *Outlook* sent an SMS. It read: 'Once in office, you had given me a pencil to jot down a few points. I didn't return it on purpose. The pencil is still with me tightly wrapped in a foil. It will remain with the things that I wish to keep forever.' In one stroke, she elevated my pencil to the status of the much sought-after pen that belonged to the character called Virus immortalized in the movie *3 Idiots* starring Aamir Khan. Notwithstanding my recent setback, what the colleague said made me feel less like an idiot and more like a warrior, primed for future battles. Bring them on …

NOTES

1: Uncovering the Cover

1. https://twitter.com/rubenbanerjee/status/1392702527368417283?lang=en, accessed on 27 January 2022.
2. https://scroll.in/latest/923004/time-magazine-cover-story-calls-pm-footntnarendra-modi-indias-divider-in-chief, accessed on 27 January 2022.
3. https://www.outlookindia.com/magazine/story/india-news-bjps-surgical-strike-on-opposition-was-part-of-a-stunning-gameplan-by-narendra-modi-amit-shah-duo/301706
4. https://twitter.com/ReshmiDG/status/1154386726602735617?s=08, accessed on 27 January 2022.
5. https://www.ndtv.com/video/news/news/pm-modi-davos-speech-india-beat-all-odds-in-coronavirus-fight-says-pm-modi-573861?rdr=1, accessed on 27 January 2022.

6. https://www.hindustantimes.com/india-news/harsh-vardhan-says-india-is-in-the-endgame-of-covid-19-pandemic-101615128329364.html, accessed on 27 January 2022.
7. https://www.ndtv.com/india-news/west-bengal-assembly-election-2021-prime-minister-narendra-modi-in-west-bengal-have-witnessed-such-a-rally-for-the-first-time-2416162, accessed on 27 January 2022.
8. https://thewire.in/health/oxygen-shortage-deaths-india-covid-19, accessed on 27 January 2022.
9. https://www.nytimes.com/2021/06/28/world/asia/india-coronavirus-oxygen.html, accessed on 27 January 2022.
10. https://www.thehindu.com/news/cities/Delhi/hc-asks-centre-why-it-should-not-face-contempt-for-failing-to-supply-oxygen-to-delhi-as-ordered/article34481630.ece, accessed on 27 January 2022.
11. https://www.outlookindia.com/magazine/issue/1
12. https://thewire.in/media/hindustan-times-bobby-ghosh-narendra-modi-shobhana-bhartia, accessed on 27 January 2022.
13. https://www.outlookindia.com/magazine/issue/11725
14. https://www.outlookindia.com/magazine/story/india-news-twice-orphaned/304535
15. https://www.outlookindia.com/magazine/story/india-news-the-empire-of-cruelty/304545
16. https://www.reuters.com/article/india-politics-khanmarket-idINKCN1T10KM, accessed on 27 January 2022.
17. https://twitter.com/mahuamoitra/status/1393127104753987584?lang=en, accessed on 27 January 2022.
18. https://www.republicworld.com/india-news/politics/bjp-releases-congress-toolkit-accuses-it-of-using-covid-19-pandemic-to-defame-pm-modi.html, accessed on 27 January 2022.

19. https://indianexpress.com/article/india/raman-singh-sambit-patra-fir-toolkit-case-7326805, accessed on 27 January 2022.
20. https://www.indiatoday.in/india/story/twitter-flags-sambit-patra-congress-toolkit-tweet-manipulated-media-1805159-2021-05-21, accessed on 27 January 2022.

2: 50 Crores Versus 50,000 Crores

1. https://www.outlookindia.com/subscription-singleissue/11726
2. https://www.outlookindia.com/subscription-singleissue/11727
3. https://www.hindustantimes.com/india-news/stain-on-india-s-human-rights-record-un-expert-on-stan-swamy-s-death-101626493982168.html, accessed on 27 January 2022
4. https://thewire.in/rights/kafeel-khan-arrest-cases-timeline, accessed on 27 January 2022.
5. https://scroll.in/article/1006767/the-siddique-kappan-case-and-the-assault-on-indias-constitution, accessed on 27 January 2022.
6. https://www.nationalheraldindia.com/india/bhima-koregaon-human-rights-bodies-must-intervene-to-help-shoma-sen-sudha-bharadwaj-get-medical-bail;see also https://indianexpress.com/article/cities/mumbai/mumbai-court-rejects-interim-bail-pleas-of-gautam-navlakha-anand-teltumbde-7467435/ and https://economictimes.indiatimes.com/news/india/delhi-riots-police-wrote-fanciful-stories-put-tadka-to-charge-sheet-umar-khalid-tells-court/articleshow/86969054.cms, all accessed on 27 January 2022.
7. https://thewire.in/rights/student-activists-natasha-narwal-devangana-kalita-uapa-delhi-police-high-court accessed on 27 January 2022.
8. https://www.newindianexpress.com/nation/2021/apr/22/evidence-planted-to-frame-activists-in-bhima-koregaon-

casesayswashington-post-report-2293138.html, accessed on 27 January 2022.

9. https://www.thehindu.com/news/national/is-this-law-necessary-sc-seeks-centres-response-on-pleas-challening-sedition-law/article35336402.ece, accessed on 27 January 2022.
10. https://www.indiatoday.in/law/story/justice-chandrachud-anti-terror-laws-misused-quell-dissent-citizens-supreme-court-1828007-2021-07-14, accessed on 27 January 2022.
11. https://www.outlookindia.com/magazine/story/india-news-opinion-justice-for-whom-laws-meant-to-fight-terror-have-become-the-real-terror/304782
12. https://www.outlookindia.com/magazine/story/india-news-law-blow-harsh-laws-are-always-used-to-suppress-dissent-and-opposition/304800
13. https://www.outlookindia.com/magazine/story/india-news-abusing-the-terror-laws-in-various-states-over-the-years/304801
14. Ibid.
15. https://www.outlookindia.com/magazine/story/india-news-the-pegasus-whodunnit/304799
16. https://indianexpress.com/article/india/dainik-bhaskar-group-it-raid-tax-evasion-7420920/ accessed on 27 January 2022.
17. https://theprint.in/india/counting-burning-buried-floating-bodies-how-dainik-bhaskar-led-national-coverage-on-covid/668941/ accessed on 27 January 2022.
18. https://www.thequint.com/news/india/how-dainik-bhaskar-led-covid-coverage-in-india, accessed on 27 January 2022.
19. https://indianexpress.com/article/india/newsclick-premises-ed-raid-editor-confined-7187683/ accessed on 27 January 2022.
20. https://www.newslaundry.com/2021/08/13/is-outlook-editor-ruben-banerjee-being-pushed-out-for-a-cover-criticising-the-government, accessed on 27 January 2022.

3: The Steep Climb

1. https://www.indiatoday.in/magazine/special-report/story/19930215-orissa-famine-drives-parents-to-sell-their-children-for-the-price-of-a-plate-of-chicken-curry-810671-1993-02-15, accessed on 27 December 2021.
2. https://www.indiatoday.in/magazine/states/story/19990125-anjana-mishra-gang-rape-case-orissa-cm-j.b.-patnaik-gets-drawn-into-the-controversy-779992-1999-01-25, accessed on 27 January 2022.
3. https://www.indiatoday.in/magazine/states/story/19981026-two-affidavits-implicate-orissa-chief-minister-in-sex-scandals-827287-1998-10-26. See also https://www.indiatoday.in/magazine/interview/story/20020513-i-am-demoralised-by-the-attitude-of-the-cbi-anjana-mishra-795199-2002-05-13, both accessed on 27 January 2022.
4. https://www.indiatoday.in/magazine/08-02-1999, accessed on 27 January 2022,
5. https://www.indiatoday.in/magazine/20-09-1999, accessed on 27 January 2022.
6. https://twitter.com/rubenbanerjee/status/1134345830981296129, accessed on 27 January 2022.
7. https://www.indiatoday.in/magazine/15-11-1999, accessed on 27 January 2022.
8. https://www.indiatoday.in/magazine/15-11-1999, accessed on 27 January 2022.
9. https://www.amazon.in/Orissa-Tragedy-Cyclones-Year-Calamity/dp/8187478217, New Delhi: Books Today, 2001.
10. https://www.indiatoday.in/magazine/22-11-1999

11. https://www.indiatoday.in/magazine/states/story/20010702-orissa-cm-naveen-patnaik-has-pmo-busy-acknowledging-his-missives-with-his-writing-skill-773708-2001-07-02
12. https://www.indiatoday.in/magazine/states/story/20001120-orissa-chief-minister-naveen-patnaiks-public-durbar-dashes-peoples-hopes-fast-778476-2000-11-20
13. https://timesofindia.indiatimes.com/india/mango-kernels-wild-roots-or-starvation-death/articleshow/1522159749.cms, accessed on 27 January 2022.
14. https://www.indiatoday.in/magazine/states/story/20021104-more-hype-than-truth-in-reports-of-hunger-related-deaths-in-orissa-794413-2002-11-04

4: Hello Habibi

1. https://www.aljazeera.com/opinions/2015/5/15/al-jazeeras-a-zaidan-i-am-a-journalist-not-terrorist, accessed on 28 January 2022.
2. https://www.egypttoday.com/Article/1/9050/22nd-anniversary-of-Hamad-bin-Khalifa-coup-on-his-father, accessed on 28 January 2022.
3. https://www.theguardian.com/media/2005/nov/23/pressandpublishing.iraq, accessed on 28 January 2022.
4. https://www.outlookindia.com/magazine/story/misguided-missiles/219769
5. https://edition.cnn.com/2003/WORLD/meast/04/08/sprj.irq.media.hit, accessed on 28 January 2022.
6. https://www.bbc.com/news/av/world-australia-31142913 accessed on 28 January 2022.
7. https://www.propublica.org/article/inside-the-campaign-to-release-dorothy-parvaz, accessed on 28 January 2022.
8. https://www.youtube.com/watch?v=iTD3Ax4XsmU

9. https://www.firstpost.com/politics/even-a-butcher-would-be-shy-of-him-lalu-attacks-narendra-modi-1501475.html
10. https://www.aljazeera.com/features/2014/6/2/sticks-and-stones accessed on 28 January 2022.
11. https://cjp.org.in/mohammed-akhlaq-lynching-case-timeline/ accessed on 28 January 2022.
12. https://www.hindustantimes.com/india-news/chhattisgarh-tv-anchor-reads-out-breaking-news-of-her-husband-s-death-in-car-accident/story-CUP5b0VlywZB646r0iPp0H.html, accessed on 28 January 2022.
13. https://twitter.com/rohitksinghlko/status/845472691628969984, accessed on 28 January 2022.
14. https://www.hindustantimes.com/india-news/escape-boredom-by-spending-a-day-in-this-220-year-old-telangana-jail-for-rs-500/story-jpdn5agPjsUU5iMNHDKE6J.html
15. https://www.hindustantimes.com/india-news/bareilly-s-14-year-old-rape-survivor-who-gave-birth-to-a-child-last-year-married-off-to-accused/story-tKGrLOfbL0JfpSghHKaWmJ.html, accessed on 28 January 2022.
16. https://www.hindustantimes.com/india-news/retracing-the-journey-of-the-jeep-with-the-human-shield-in-kashmir-s-budgam/story-hKIE1l73JF76CCzlfpNf4L.html, accessed on 28 January 2022
17. https://www.bbc.com/news/world-asia-india-40008876, accessed on 28 January 2022.
18. https://www.hindustantimes.com/india-news/retracing-the-journey-of-the-jeep-with-the-human-shield-in-kashmir-s-budgam/story-hKIE1l73JF76CCzlfpNf4L.html, accessed on 28 January 2022.
19. https://www.greaterkashmir.com/kashmir/army-chief-assures-stern-action-against-kashmir-human-shield-major-leetul-gogoi, accessed on 28 January 2022

20. https://www.thehindu.com/news/national/pehlu-khan-lynching-case-hc-issues-warrants-against-accused/article36335623.ece, accessed on 28 January 2022.
21. https://caravanmagazine.in/media/history-repeating-shobhana-bhartias-hindustan-times, accessed on 28 January 2022.

5: An Inlook

1. *Outlook*, 12 March 2018.
2. Worst Chief Minister: *Outlook*, 16 June 2014; Best Chief Minister: *Outlook*, 4 September 2017.
3. https://www.outlookindia.com/magazine/story/dad-writ-large/290992
4. https://www.outlookindia.com/magazine/story/the-art-of-speaking/299234
5. https://www.indiatoday.in/magazine/cover-story/story/19950115-carrying-hope-754340-1995-01-15, accessed on 29 January 2022.
6. https://www.outlookindia.com/magazine/issue/11601
7. https://www.outlookindia.com/magazine/story/issue-of-the-year-menstruation-why-it-was-the-natural-choice/301037
8. Basingstoke: Palgrave Macmillan, 2013.
9. https://www.outlookindia.com/magazine/issue/11612
10. https://www.outlookindia.com/magazine/issue/11614
11. https://www.outlookindia.com/magazine/issue/11615
12. https://www.outlookindia.com/magazine/issue/11665
13. https://www.outlookindia.com/magazine/issue/11672
14. https://www.outlookindia.com/magazine/story/india-news-the-hateras-and-us/303787
15. https://thewire.in/government/parliament-apology-deaths-second-covid-19-wave-manoj-jha-rjd, accessed on 29 January 2022.

6: The Immorality of Moral Clarity

1. Rana Ayyub, *Gujarat Files: Anatomy of a Cover Up*, self-published, 2016.
2. https://www.thehindu.com/books/literary-review/An-unfinished-book/article14384513.ece , accessed on 29 January 2022.
3. https://www.business-standard.com/article/economy-policy/unemployment-rate-at-five-decade-high-of-6-1-in-2017-18-nsso-survey-119013100053_1.html, accessed on 29 January 2022.
4. https://www.theleaflet.in/unemployment-crisis-is-reaching-the-stage-of-social-explosion-leaked-nsso-report-is-fabulous-journalism-and-a-wake-up-call/, accessed on 29 January 2022.
5. https://www.outlookindia.com/magazine/issue/11658
6. https://www.outlookindia.com/magazine/issue/11658
7. https://thewire.in/rights/farmers-protest-godi-media-channels-ground-reporters, accessed on 29 January 2022
8. https://www.ndtv.com/india-news/jnu-students-union-president-attacked-on-campus-violence-breaks-out-2159160, accessed on 29 January 2022.]
9. https://www.outlookindia.com/website/story/india-news-jnu-a-microcosm-of-india-it-continues-to-academically-excel-despite-all-backlash-aishe-ghosh/354726
10. https://www.outlookindia.com/website/story/opinion-jnu-must-get-rid-of-anti-national-forces-to-transform-into-centre-of-educational-excellence/354797
11. https://www.outlookindia.com/website/story/opinion-dear-editor-i-disagree-with-your-both-sides-journalism/354922
12. https://www.outlookindia.com/website/story/opinion-impartial-media-the-truth-lies-only-in-both-sides-journalism/355048

13. https://www.outlookindia.com/magazine/story/india-news-opinion-lutyens-medias-attempt-to-paint-the-anti-caa-agitation-as-secular-was-hypocritic/302847, accessed on 28 January 2022.
14. https://www.outlookindia.com/subscription-singleissue/11189
15. https://www.outlookindia.com/magazine/issue/11728
16. https://www.hindustantimes.com/india-news/before-2017-ration-went-to-those-who-used-to-say-abba-jaan-up-cm-yogi-101631468843980.html, accessed on 28 January 2022.
17. https://www.outlookindia.com/magazine/issue/11661
18. https://www.thehindu.com/news/cities/mumbai/actor-sushant-singh-rajput-found-dead-in-mumbai/article31826151.ece, accessed on 29 January 2022.
19. https://www.freepressjournal.in/umbai/rhea-chakraborty-arrested-ncb-terms-her-as-active-member-of-drug-syndicate, accessed on 29 January 2022.
20. https://www.bbc.com/news/world-asia-india-53932725, accessed on 29 January.
21. https://indianexpress.com/article/explained/three-crore-indians-use-cannabis-ganja-in-northeast-bhang-elsewhere-5599281/, accessed on 29 January.
22. https://www.outlookindia.com/website/story/india-news-with-justice-for-sushant-hashtag-vulgar-bhojpuri-songs-target-rhea-chakraborty/359991, accessed on 1 December 2021.
23. https://www.outlookindia.com/magazine/issue/11689
24. https://www.outlookindia.com/magazine/story/india-news-daily-noose/303655
25. https://www.news18.com/news/politics/the-sunanda-tharoor-case-trial-by-the-media-719557.html, accessed on 15 November 2021.
26. https://www.editorji.com/story/sunanda-pushkar-death-case-mystery-media-trial-and-clean-chit-to-shashi-tharoor-1629316896265, accessed on 29 January.

27. https://www.thequint.com/news/india/tharoor-gets-clean-chit-in-pushkar-case-but-time-for-action-against-media-trials, accessed on 29 January.
28. https://www.thehindu.com/news/national/india-again-placed-at-142nd-rank-in-press-freedom/article34377079.ece#:~:text=The%202021%20World%20Press%20Freedom,rank%20out%20of%20180%20countries,accessed on 29 January 2022.
29. https://thewire.in/media/india-today-tanushree-pandey-hathras-case-phone-tapping
30. https://thewire.in/media/summoned-raided-censored-crackdown-on-journalists-is-the-new-normal-in-kashmir, accessed on 29 January 2022.
31. https://www.economist.com/leaders/2021/09/04/the-threat-from-the-illiberal-left, accessed on 29 January 2022.

7: Weaponization of News

1. https://www.outlookindia.com/newsscroll/pm-allows-priyanka-gandhis-request-to-stay-on-in-lutyens-bungalow-for-some-time-ians-special/1894775
2. https://www.outlookindia.com/newsscroll/pm-allows-priyanka-gandhis-request-to-stay-on-in-lutyens-bungalow-for-some-time-ians-special/1894775
3. https://www.altnews.in/ians-media-outlets-fall-for-fake-twitter-account-of-sushant-singh-rajputs-father/?utm_source=website&utm_medium=social-media&utm_campaign=newpost, accessed on 2 February 2022.
4. https://www.altnews.in/ians-media-outlets-fall-for-fake-twitter-account-of-sushant-singh-rajputs-father/?utm_source=website&utm_medium=social-media&utm_campaign=newpost, accessed on 2 February 2022.

5. https://www.outlookindia.com/newsscroll/chorus-grows-for-cbi-inquiry-into-sushants-death/1886648
6. https://time.com/5815264/coronavirus-india-islamophobia-coronajihad/, accessed on 2 February 2022
7. https://indianexpress.com/article/opinion/editorials/tablighi-jamaat-covid-19-coronavirus-delhi-police-7107751/, accessed on 2 February 2022.
8. https://www.aninews.in/news/world/asia/pakistan-sponsored-elements-and-khalistan-sympathisers-actively-involved-in-farmers-protest20210129084252/ , accessed on 2 February 2022.
9. https://www.dnaindia.com/india/report-dna-explainer-how-khalistan-supporters-are-conspiring-to-use-farmers-protest-to-unleash-mayhem-in-india-2877111, accessed on 2 February 2022.
10. https://twitter.com/priyankagandhi/status/1282886260915228678, accessed on 2 February 2022.
11. https://twitter.com/hardeepspuri/status/1282929364707864576?s=21, accessed on 2 February 2022.
12. https://twitter.com/hardeepspuri/status/1282952207466291200?s=21, accessed on 2 February 2022.
13. https://twitter.com/hardeepspuri/status/1282952209722793984?s=21, accessed on 2 February 2022.
14. https://www.altnews.in/right-wingers-pass-off-guatemalan-mob-lynching-video-one-marwadi-woman-burnt-alive-muslim-mob/, accessed on 2 February 2022.
15. https://www.latestly.com/socially/india/news/the-outlook-group-has-terminated-the-services-of-group-editor-in-chief-ruben-banerjee-latest-tweet-by-ians-tweets-2851756.html, accessed on 2 February 2022.
16. https://theshillongtimes.com/2021/09/15/outlook-terminates-services-of-group-editor-in-chief-ruben-banerjee/, accessed on 2 February 2022.

17. https://www.exchange4media.com/media-print-news/outlook-sacks-its-group-editor-in-chief-ruben-banerjee-115696.html, accessed on 2 February 2022.
18. https://reutersinstitute.politics.ox.ac.uk/digital-news-report/2021/india, accessed on 2 February 2022.
19. https://caravanmagazine.in/media/government-punishment-dainik-bhaskar-bravery, accessed on 2 February.
20. https://theprint.in/india/india-is-now-only-partly-free-freedom-in-the-world-report-downgrades-status/615481/, accessed on 2 February 2022.
21. https://www.thehindu.com/news/national/india-again-placed-at-142nd-rank-in-press-freedom/article34377079.ece , accessed on 2 February 2022.
22. https://www.thenewsminute.com/article/nbdsa-finds-times-now-zee-news-violated-ethics-code-157923, accessed on 2 February 2022.
23. https://indianexpress.com/article/business/ad-revenue-facebook-and-google-make-more-than-top-10-media-firms-put-together-7655241/, accessed on 2 February 2022.
24. https://caravanmagazine.in/vantage/death-of-judge-loya-supreme-court-examination-ecg-post-mortem-demonstrates-failings-judgment, accessed on 2 February 2022.
25. https://www.indiatoday.in/india/story/judge-loya-case-a-tale-of-twists-and-turns-before-supreme-court-says-full-stop-1215513-2018-04-19, accessed on 5 February 2022.
26. https://theprint.in/opinion/a-hurried-move-in-judge-loya-case-can-only-make-amit-shah-more-powerful/349420/, accessed on 5 February 2022.
27. https://www.freepressjournal.in/india/what-is-the-justice-loya-case-and-how-is-amit-shah-involved, accessed on 5 February 2022.

28. https://indianexpress.com/article/opinion/columns/uttar-pradesh-yogi-adityanath-four-years-of-govt-economy-coronavirus-governance-7234766/, accessed on 5 February 2022.

8: The Endgame

1. https://indianexpress.com/article/india/what-is-the-bofors-scandal-case-why-is-it-being-opened-now-4823576/, accessed on 2 February 2022.
2. https://www.nytimes.com/1981/08/11/world/price-of-woman-in-india-306-and-much-sorrow.html, accessed on 2 February 2022.
3. https://scroll.in/article/822500/dilip-padgaonkar-1944-2016-the-man-who-held-the-second-most-important-job-in-the-country, accessed on 2 February 2022.
4. https://www.newslaundry.com/2021/08/13/is-outlook-editor-ruben-banerjee-being-pushed-out-for-a-cover-criticising-the-government, accessed on 2 February 2022.
5. https://theprint.in/india/outlook-group-editor-in-chief-sacked-2-hours-after-rejoining-work-commissioning-cover-on-yogi/734109/, accessed on 2 February 2022.
6. https://thefederal.com/news/outlooks-missing-editor-sacked-after-spate-of-anti-modi-govt-stories/, accessed on 2 February 2022.
7. https://www.newsclick.in/Did-Abba-Jaan-Lead-Outlook-Editor-Exit, accessed on 2 February 2022.
8. https://www.newslaundry.com/2021/09/17/why-did-outlook-get-a-new-editor-and-sack-ruben-banerjee, accessed on 2 February 2022.
9. Vinod Mehta, *Lucknow Boy: A Memoir*, New Delhi: Penguin Viking, 2011, pp. 202–03. See also https://thewire.in/media/

outlooks-owner-raided-vajpayees-time-media-response-quite-different, accessed on 2 February 2022

10. https://www.outlookindia.com/website/story/this-is-an-income-tax-raid/211800, accessed on 2 February 2022.
11. https://twitter.com/newslaundry/status/1137304909752094720, accessed on 2 February 2022.
12. https://caravanmagazine.in/media/personal-history-outlook-magazine, accessed on 2 February 2022.
13. https://www.facebook.com/sajjan.k.singh, accessed on 2 February 2022.

ACKNOWLEDGEMENTS

THE CREDIT FOR THIS BOOK GOES TO SEVERAL PEOPLE, BUT THE foremost among them is Swati Chopra, executive editor at HarperCollins. From the day I first pitched the idea for this book, her support has been unstinted. From hurrying up the book contract to meticulously going through the manuscript, which she diligently edited, she has nurtured this book with utmost care. A big thank you, Swati.

I am also grateful to the others at HarperCollins, including my copy editor Antony Thomas. His editorial interventions helped this book enormously and I truly appreciate them.

Saurav Das, the resident creative genius at HarperCollins, deserves a special mention. His cover design made an enormous difference to the book.

There have been several journalist-friends who have contributed in no small measure in giving shape to this book.

Besides brainstorming with me, they have helped me all through with useful perspectives and important suggestions. I am not naming them since making public their help might professionally inconvenience them. But they know who they are and I gratefully tip my hat to them.

Last but not the least, I am grateful to my family – wife Amrita and daughter Rupsa – for putting up with me. That task, I guess, is no less than writing a book.

INDEX

ABOUT THE AUTHOR

Ruben Banerjee was the editor-in-chief at Outlook group during one of the most challenging times faced by the Indian media and there was never a dull moment. Even the manner in which his editorship ended was eventful, adding further drama to a long career characterized by many twists and turns.

Having started out as a reporter with *Newstime*, the now-defunct daily in Hyderabad, he worked across several states – first as a reporter with the *Indian Express* and then for *India Today*. He later went abroad and worked with Al Jazeera for twelve years in Doha, Qatar.

On returning and before taking over the reins at *Outlook*, he led the countrywide news network of *Hindustan Times* as its national affairs editor.

This is his third book, after *The Orissa Tragedy: A Cyclone's Year of Calamity* and *Naveen Patnaik*, an unauthorized biography of the Odisha chief minister.

P
6-6-22